SOCIAL MEDIA MONSTERS: Internet Killers

RJ Parker
JJ Slate

SOCIAL MEDIA MONSTERS: Internet Killers

ISBN-13: 978-1500959197
ISBN-10: 1500959197

Authored by

RJ Parker
JJ Slate

Edited by: Hartwell Editing
Cover design by: Jacqueline Cross

License Notes

Contents

Introduction

Murder. Kidnapping. Cannibalism. Suicide. All of these themes can be found in the following thirty-three true stories about various killers who have used the internet to locate, lure, stalk, or exploit their victims. As you read through the case files of this book, you will learn about the shocking lives led by online predators from all around the world.

This book is written in a way to help you understand the killer better by exposing his or her background and, if the information is available, the reasons that led the killer to commit the murders. These types of murderers are identified as people who are motivated by a psychological factor: some murderers are triggered by anger or jealousy, others kill as a way to seek attention, and some are merely in it for the thrill of the kill. Unfortunately, sometimes the real reasons behind the murderous acts you will read about in this book are not always known or understood.

These stories bring to light that any person can fall victim to an online killer, even if the perpetrator is living on the other half of the earth. How can you protect yourself from such dangers? In the last chapter of the book, we'll talk about the importance of online privacy and how to avoid sharing personal information online, a potentially dangerous and deadly act.

You will learn how killers are using all sorts of online networks to lure their victims, such as Craigslist, Facebook, chat rooms, and other social media sites. You will also learn about some cases where people have teamed up together to commit the murders.

At the end of each story, you will find the outcome of the stories, including their arrests, trials, and sometimes deaths. Thorough research has been made, drawing on many various resources, to come up with an accurate string of events defining the background, the crimes, and the aftermath of the killer's life. As you continue reading, keep in mind that these are real people and real events.

While this book focuses on killers who use social media to assist in their killing, it's important to note that the era of the internet didn't create these types of killers; they have always been around. The internet and the many variations of social media may have just made it easier for today's killers to find their victims. A few of the more notorious killers of this nature are briefly highlighted next.

The Lonely Hearts Killers
In the era before the internet, killers were known to use want ads in the newspaper to locate their victims. Raymond Martinez Fernandez and Martha Beck were a serial killer couple dubbed the "Lonely Hearts Killers," or the "Honeymoon Killers," who killed as many as twenty different women during 1947 and 1949 they met through the Lonely Heart ads they posted in local newspapers. Raymond was born on December 17, 1914. He served as a merchant marine in World War II, but on his return home after the war, he suffered a skull fracture in an accident aboard the ship. He spent three months in the hospital and when he was sent home, he was a changed man. Some believe it was

this head injury that turned him into a cold-blooded murderer.

After the war, he began writing letters to women who had posted ads in the Lonely Hearts section of the newspaper. When he met the women in person, he would rob them of their money, jewelry, and other belongings. The women would often be too ashamed to call the police on Raymond and he was able to con many vulnerable women this way.

It is believed Raymond's first murder was a woman he dated for a brief time. Jane Lucilla Thompson was found dead in a hotel room in Spain after the couple traveled there together. Police were unable to determine her cause of death. Raymond was able to obtain all of her money and belongings by forging her signature on a will.

Raymond also met Martha Beck through a Lonely Hearts ad in the personals section of a newspaper. The two wrote letters together while Raymond lived in New York and Martha lived in Florida. They met for the first time in 1947, when Raymond traveled to Florida to visit her. Raymond told

Martha about how he often met women through the Lonely Hearts ads and robbed them. The two teamed up and began scamming women together, with Martha posing as his sister or sister-in-law.

The crimes soon escalated into murder. They began killing together and discovered they enjoyed it. Their first victim was Janet Fay. Martha hit Janet in the skull with a hammer after catching her in bed with Raymond, who then strangled her to death. The murderous couple went on to kill as many as seventeen women, as well as the infant of one of their victims.

Thanks to the quick thinking of a suspicious neighbor living next door to one of their victims, the police zeroed in on the killer couple squatting in the house and brought them into the station for questioning on February 28, 1949. There, they admitted their crimes and signed a seventy-three-page confession.

The couple put to death on the same day by the electric chair at Sing Sing prison in New York on March 8, 1951. Raymond was executed first, and his lover was executed shortly after.

The Want Ad Killer

Harvey Carignan was born on May 18, 1927. He lived a troubled childhood, compounded with behavioral problems and bedwetting. When he was eight years old, his mother sent him to live with his aunt and uncle, who quickly sent him back home. When he was ten, he was sent to live with his grandmother, who soon sent him to another aunt's house. When he ran away to live with his mother again, she attempted to put him in an orphanage. He was finally sent to a reform school at age twelve, where he remained until he was eighteen years old. He later claimed that female employees at the reform school sexually abused him. As soon as he turned eighteen, Harvey enlisted in the army, where he was stationed in Anchorage, Alaska.

In 1949, he was sentenced to death by hanging in Alaska for raping and murdering a woman named Laura Showatler. His death sentence was reversed, however, after his lawyers were able to convince the courts that his confession had been coerced. He was released on parole in 1960, where he continued to get into trouble with the law for various crimes, such as burglary and assault. In 1973, Harvey posted an ad looking for employees to work for him at his service station. A young girl named Kathy Miller responded to his ad. Her remains were found a month later, wrapped in a sheet of plastic and discarded in an Indian reservation in Washington State. Her head had been bashed in with a hammer. It was this killing that later earned Harvey the nicknames "The Want Ad Killer" and "Harv the Hammer."

He fled the state after this crime and over the next year, Harvey kidnapped several women and picked up female hitchhikers, attacking them with a hammer and sexually assaulting them. He released some of them when he was finished with them and several women were actually able to escape. Others were not so lucky. It is believed he killed at least five women and raped ten others before 1974, when he was finally caught.

At his trial, Harvey pleaded not guilty by reason of insanity. He was ultimately diagnosed with severe antisocial personality disorder. He was found guilty of sodomy for the brutal attacks of two women, Jerri Billings and Gwen Burton, and received a total sentence of sixty years in prison, but due to Minnesota's laws he was only ordered to serve forty of those years. He was later indicted for the murder of three more women, Kathy Miller, Eileen Hunley, and Katherine Schultz. He pleaded guilty to those murders, racking up 150 years in prison in all, but ultimately he will only serve forty years and could be paroled as early as 2015. However, he developed prostate cancer in 1997 at the age of seventy-two, and it has been reported he is in fairly poor health.

The Classified Ad Rapist
Bobby Joe Long was born on October 14, 1953 in West Virginia. Before the age of ten, he had been hit by a car on two separate occasions, both times suffering major head injuries. He was born with an extra x chromosome, which reportedly led to his developing of breasts during his teenage years. He also had an unnatural relationship with his

mother, who worked as a bartender, and he slept in her bed with her until he was thirteen years old.

In 1981, he began answering classified ads placed by women selling various appliances and furniture. When he entered a home and could determine that the woman was home alone, he would rape her. He later began contacting women through the *Penny Saver* and other classified ads and raped at least fifty different women in this manner. He also liked to prowl neighborhoods, looking for women home alone with "For Sale" signs on their front lawns.

In 1984, Bobby went on an eight-month killing spree, killing at least ten prostitutes and hitchhikers he had picked up. He was arrested in November 1984 and received two death sentences. He remains on death row in Florida to this day, awaiting execution.

While the Lonely Hearts Killers, the Want Ad Killer, and the Classified Ad Rapist Killer all committed their crimes long before the internet became available, the types of crimes they committed and the methods they used to locate their victims are very similar to some of those you are about to read.

Chapter 1: Armin Meiwes

The internet has made everyday tasks so much easier. For example, with only a few clicks, you can shop for clothes, groceries, and even order a meal to be delivered to you. Armin Meiwes used the internet to order an unusual kind of food: human flesh!

Armin Meiwes was born on December 1, 1961 in Kassel, Germany. His parents were rarely interested in their son, so Armin grew up as a lonely child. When he was eight years old, his parents broke up and his father left him alone with his mother. Growing up, Armin was a good boy, obsessed with the story "Hansel and Gretel" by the Brothers Grimm. His favorite chapter was when Hansel was being fed up in preparation to be cooked and eaten.

Armin's mother was controlling. She would accompany him everywhere and would often yell at him in public. However, she was not really interested in her son's life, so Armin created an imaginary brother whom he named "Franky" and with whom he discussed his thoughts. Franky, unlike his mother, would listen to him. At age twelve, Armin developed the unnatural desire to eat his friends so they would stay with him forever.

In 1999, Armin's mother passed away when he was thirty-eight. The computer repair technician was left alone in the large family mansion in Amstetten. In the house, Armin made a shrine for his mother. Her room was left untouched and Armin placed a mannequin made of plastic in her bed to pretend she was still there with him. During that time, Armin became interested in pornography, especially the type that included torture.

Armin's obsession with torturous pornographic videos on the internet led him to a site called The Cannibal Café. The people participating in the site's chat rooms were interested in cannibalism. Although the site had a disclaimer that made it clear that it was all just fantasies, for Armin it was the perfect place to meet his victim.

In the year 2000, Armin posted one message in which he stated that he was searching for "a young, well-built man aged 18 to 30 years old to be slaughtered and then consumed...If you are 18-25, you are my boy...come to me, I'll eat your delicious flesh." Armin received many responses to the post, but most of them did not go all the way. One of them was from a man named Borg Jose. Borg met with Armin, but as he lay on the table waiting to be slaughtered, he suddenly asked to be released because he felt sick. Armin let him go.

The last man to reply to Armin's post was a forty-three-year-old engineer named Bernd-Jürgen Brandes. Bernd was openly bisexual. On February 14, 2001, Bernd contacted Armin and agreed to volunteer to be eaten by him. Bernd posted, "I offer myself to you and will let you dine from my live body." Over the next few days, Armin and Bernd exchanged messages as they discussed how Armin should eat Bernd and what Armin should do with his body afterwards. Bernd gave many suggestions; one of them was that his skull could be used as an ashtray. Bernd asked if he was the first one to be killed and eaten by Armin, and Armin

13

told him that indeed he was.

On March 9, 2001, Bernd went to Armin's house. They kissed, had sex, and then Armin gave Bernd sleeping pills, Vicks cough medicine, and some alcohol. Then, Armin tried to chew off Bernd's penis but couldn't, so Bernd put his penis on the table while Armin cut it off. Bernd tried to eat his own penis raw, but determined it was too "chewy." This was when Armin put it in a pan in an attempt to fry it with garlic, salt, pepper, and some of Bernd's fat so the two could dine on it together. However, he burned the dish, making it inedible, so Armin instead fed it to his dog. During this time, Bernd's injuries caused him to lose a tremendous amount of blood. Armin put him in the bathtub and read a *Star Trek* book for the next three hours as Bernd slowly lost more and more blood. Bernd stayed alive for the next ten hours. Finally, Armin stabbed Bernd in the neck several times and killed him, ending his pain.

Death was not the end for Bernd. Armin hung his corpse on a meat hook and began cutting it into smaller chunks. He even tried to grind the bones of his victim into flour. The entire body was dismembered and the pieces were stored in his freezer. For the next ten months, Armin defrosted and ate pieces of Bernd's flesh. He had also videotaped himself murdering Bernd and dismembering his body.

By the month of November of 2002, Armin's supply of human flesh was almost finished. He started looking for another victim. Like the last time, Armin posted on the site a message detailing his request, this time adding more details about his intentions. An Austrian student saw the post and reported it to the police. On December 11, 2002, the police burst into Armin's house where they found the remaining flesh of Bernd along with a video of the murder and cannibalism and many pictures of pornography and torture. Armin was arrested and immediately confessed to the murder. For seven months, the police worked on constructing a case against him, while searching Armin's computer for more evidence.

On July 17, 2003, Armin was charged with murder. It was a controversial trial, as many believed since Bernd had volunteered to be killed and eaten, Armin hadn't forced him to do anything. On January 30, 2004, Armin was convicted of manslaughter. He received a sentence of eight and a half years in prison. However, in April 2005, the court ordered a retrial. Prosecutors argued that Armin should be convicted of murder. During the retrial in January 2006, they highlighted how Armin's motives satisfied his sexual desires. They also argued that Bernd was not able to make decisions since he was drunk and under the effects of drugs. On May 10, 2006, Armin's sentence was changed to life imprisonment.

Chapter 2: Michael John Anderson

Since the internet came into being, many have used various websites to find employment. Craigslist is a classified advertisements website that includes many sections for jobs, wanted items or services, housing, and much more; that is why it came as a huge surprise to the public when, in October 2007, Michael John Anderson ordered a murder victim through Craigslist. He was the first murderer to be referred to as the "Craigslist Killer."

Michael was studying auto mechanics in Cedar Alternative High School located in Eagan, Minnesota, but he dropped out. He worked for a while in various auto parts warehouses. A few months before his arrest in 2007, he was working the night shift at the Minneapolis St. Paul Airport, refueling jets.

Michael was living with his parents in his family's home in Savage. He had two other siblings older than him. At the time, his father was laid off from Northwest Airlines where he had once worked as a mechanic.

Not much is known about the childhood and early life of Michael, but he was known as a nice kid. He had friends with whom he used to play video games. Michael was shy around women. No one expected him to grow into a man who would hurt anyone. He was perceived as a normal guy.

Until now, there is no apparent reason to explain why Michael planned the murder of twenty-four-year-old Katherine Ann Olson. He only wanted to experience the feeling of killing someone. Fortunately, Michael did not plan ahead and he was caught early on in his murderous career before he could inflict more pain.

Using Craigslist, Michael posted an advertisement asking for a nanny. He pretended to be a woman named 'Amy.' The unlucky responder was Katherine Olson. Katherine had graduated from St. Olaf College in 2006. She had a degree in theater and Hispanic studies. She also worked as a temporary nanny. On Thursday, October 25, 2007, after many emails exchanged between Katherine and 'Amy,' Katherine went to meet her new employer who had asked her to babysit from 10:30 a.m. to 5:00 p.m. Before leaving, Katherine told her roommate that she thought her new employer seemed a bit strange, but she was going to show up for the job anyway. After all, Katherine had answered two previous ads on Craigslist and had worked as a nanny at least twice before.

Katherine thought that she was going to meet a woman or a couple. To her surprise, Michael was the one who answered the door. Somehow, he got her upstairs where he shot her in her back with a .357 Magnum. The autopsy later revealed that Katherine bled for fifteen minutes after being shot. She also sustained other injuries when Michael dragged her body downstairs, stuffed her into a sleeping bag, and threw her in the trunk of her own car. He drove her body to the Burnsville Nature Preserve, five blocks away from his house, and abandoned the car there.

Katherine's purse was found in a dumpster the next day and turned over to the police. When investigators called Katherine's residence to notify her that her purse had been found, her roommate answered and told them that Katherine had not come home from a babysitting job the day before. A search was initiated. With the help of a helicopter, police located her vehicle at the nature preserve. To their horror, they found her corpse in the trunk of the car with her ankles bound. In a nearby garbage can, they located Katherine's smashed cell phone wrapped in some bloody towels. One of the towels had Michael's name on it.

The address and phone number of 'Amy' were those of Michael's address and phone number. In addition, the email used by 'Amy' was traced back to Michael. The evidence was overwhelming. Upon searching Michael's house, investigators located blood that matched Katherine's, especially on the stairs where drag marks were still visible. In Michael's bedroom, a gun and some shell casings were found. Blood spatter was found on the walls and on the mattress as well. Moreover, a neighbor had seen Katherine's car in front of Michael's house for more than two hours on Thursday, the day of the murder. There was no evidence that indicated that Michael and Katherine knew each other prior to their encounter the day of the murder. Also, there was not any evidence of sexual assault.

Nineteen-year-old Michael was arrested at his workplace. At first, he denied any involvement in the murder. He claimed that he had not used Craigslist personally since January of that year but his mother and other three friends had access to his account. He also claimed that he had never contacted the victim. Despite these claims, there was just too much evidence incriminating him. When the police confronted him with the evidence that they had found, Michael claimed that he was present at the time of the murder, but actually a friend had committed the slaying, thinking that "it would be funny."

Michael was charged with one count of first-degree premeditated murder, and one count of second-degree intentional murder. The defense claimed that Michael suffered from Asperger syndrome, a form of autism. However, after examination, it was revealed that Michael was not mentally ill. In addition to all the physical evidence, the prosecution highlighted the fact that Michael never told the police that the shooting was an accident. He never seemed sorry for what he had done. During the trial, Michael did not testify and he expressed no remorse for his crimes. On April 1, 2009, Michael was found guilty of both charges, in addition to second-degree manslaughter, and was sentenced to life imprisonment without the chance of parole.

Chapter 3: John Steven Burgess

In 2007, Donna Jou was a beautiful nineteen-year-old pre-med student at San Diego State University. A dedicated student, Donna hoped to become a doctor someday so she could care for elderly patients. She volunteered at battered women's shelters and food drives. She was always trying to help others in need and wanted to spend the rest of her life doing just that. In June of 2007, she was spending her summer break at her parents' home in Rancho Santa Margarita, California. Looking to make some extra cash, she placed an ad on Craigslist offering math tutoring.

A thirty-six-year-old man named John Steven Burgess responded to her ad. According to court documents, he described himself as "a loving father, a devoted son, and a decorated veteran of Desert Storm." What Donna didn't know was that he was a convicted sex offender. In 2002, John (then thirty-one) had been convicted of battery and committing a lewd act on a girl younger than fourteen. He served a 146-day prison sentence and was released on the condition he register as a sex offender, which he never did. In 2005, he was arrested for assault after attacking his ex-girlfriend.

Donna and John struck up an online relationship. They spent nearly a month emailing each other, discussing things like school and family. John later claimed Donna told him she had always wanted to try drugs. It was then he invited her to a party at his house.

On June 23, 2007, Donna's mother, Nili Jou, last saw her daughter as she hopped onto the back of John's motorcycle, headed to his house in Los Angeles. She had no way of knowing that would be the last time she would ever see her daughter alive. When Donna didn't return home the next day, Nili immediately called police.

When the authorities came knocking on his door, John refused to cooperate. Soon after, he painted his pickup truck, stole some money from his roommate, and moved to Florida. He began using an alias, Logan Anderson, as he tried to avoid the police. On

July 9, investigators located a black toolbox that John had once kept in the back of his truck. Inside, they discovered a rope, rubber gloves, a scrub brush, and his truck's license plate, reading SINJIN1. When investigators finally caught up with him in Florida, John was arrested on drug charges and failure to register as a sex offender for his prior conviction.

Donna's parents wouldn't get any answers about their daughter's whereabouts for two more years. In May of 2009, John finally pleaded guilty to involuntary manslaughter and told police his version of what happened that night. He claimed that when the two arrived at his home in Palms, he gave Donna cocaine, heroin, and alcohol. When he woke the next morning, he allegedly found her dead in a chair, covered with her own vomit. He claimed he wrapped her in a few sheets and stuffed her into his military duffel bag. He put her body in the back of his truck and then drove to the ocean. "I went down to my sailboat and gave her to the sea," he told police.

John told investigators exactly where he

claimed to have dumped Donna's body in the ocean, but an extensive search turned up empty. Her remains have never been found. Donna's relatives do not believe that she accepted drugs and overdosed, as John claims. They cannot accept her death and cling to the morbid hope that she might be alive and being held captive somewhere. They have even hired a private investigator to look for her. "I read these stories about people being found after so many years, and I'm just hoping I'm one of those lucky ones," Nili once told reporters.

John was given a five-year prison sentence after pleading guilty to involuntary manslaughter, of which he only served about two years before he was released on parole. Donna's family was outraged.

In July of 2012, two women called the police on John again. According to reports, they both responded to a Craigslist ad posted by a man named "Johnny" promising a rent-free room in his apartment in exchange for cooking and cleaning. The two women, who didn't know each other before responding to the ad, both visited the apartment to meet

26

with John on the same day. John began to tell them a rambling "true story" about his life and Donna Jou's death after he learned that they were writers. He told the women after he found Donna dead in his house, he put her body in a trashcan and dumped it in the ocean. While they were in the apartment, they also caught glimpse of a woman who appeared to be groggy, dressed only in underwear, and trembling uncontrollably. Troubled by 'Johnny's' story, the two women Googled his name when they got home and decided to go to authorities when they realized he was an ex-convict. He was arrested on possession of ammunition and violating his parole, which prohibited him from using social media and the internet to meet women. He pleaded no contest to being a felon in possession of ammunition and was sentenced to four years in prison soon after.

When Nili Jou heard of John's arrest, she told a KTLA reporter that she was relieved. She said she and her husband had feared he would kill again once he was out of prison and she was thankful he was back behind bars.

John was imprisoned at Chuckawalla Valley State Prison in Riverside County for just two years. He was released on July 24, 2014 on the condition he register as a sex offender and wear a GPS tracking device. Donna Jou's parents reached out to the media again, this time hoping to warn everyone in his neighborhood about his past. Nili planned on making fliers and distributing them to everyone in the area. "He got away with murder," she told reporters. "I'm afraid and I'm sure he's going to do it again."

Chapter 4: Christian Grotheer

Over the past few decades, the internet has become widely used. Although the benefits the internet has provided for the human race are uncountable, there are many disadvantages offered as well, including those that are deadly. And these dangers don't just exist in one country; they are spread throughout the world. Stalkers, rapists, and killers have all found new avenues to commit crimes through the internet, and the victims are falling in piles. One of the countries affected by this nightmarish spread of crime is Germany, where the first internet killer there "graduated" in 2008.

Christian Grotheer was a construction laborer. His father was very abusive and this made Christian's childhood a disaster. As a young boy, Christian had to be taken into the care of child protective services because of his father. Christian recalls one time, at the age of six, he saw his father raping his mother who was screaming and calling for help. This event was very traumatic for him.

Growing up, Christian started taking drugs, but then found something else to which he became addicted: online chat rooms. He claimed that chatting over the internet helped him overcome his drug addiction. He spent most nights chatting with strangers over the internet. He claims to have actually met around 100 women face-to-face after chatting with them for a while and even had sexual contact with some of them. It was through these chat rooms that Christian would meet his two victims.

Christian was using the online nicknames 'Rosenboy0207' and 'Riddick300' in the online chat rooms where he met various women. On June 5, 2008, Christian met with Jessica K. who was using the online nickname 'babylove.' Jessica was twenty-six years old at the time, the same age as Christian. Fourteen days after their meeting, Jessica's body was found. Christian (after his arrest) claimed that he and Jessica had gotten into an argument that quickly turned into a heated fight. He claimed that he had only "touched her on the throat," and then she had dropped dead. Traces of Jessica's blood were found on Christian's shoes, but he said that the source was from a nosebleed Jessica had gotten while they were still walking together. The prosecution claimed that Christian had stabbed Jessica in the back, but Jessica's corpse was already in the process of decomposing when she was discovered and the cause of death could not actually be determined.

Only twelve days after Jessica's murder, on June 17, 2008, Christian claimed his second victim from the chat room. He met up with Regina B., a mother of three children. According to Christian, the two had sex in Regina's apartment. Then Regina cooked a meal for them. After that, they went to walk her dog. Christian claims that Regina demanded that he pay her a sum of money and enter into a serious relationship with her, or she would report him to the police, claiming that he had raped her. When Regina called him a rapist, Christian claimed he had a flashback to the time his father raped his mother while she screamed for help. Filled with anger, Christian recalled that he saw "the eyes of Jesus." He then attacked Regina with a kitchen knife and stabbed her twenty-six times: twelve times in her back, and fourteen times in her chest. Her body was found the next day when a passerby discovered her. Christian told police that if it wasn't for her calling him a rapist, Regina would probably still be alive. He claimed to have been driven by fear and anger and that he didn't feel in control at the time of the murder. Christian never took the blame for his actions; instead he blamed the victim and his traumatic childhood.

Christian's defense tried to portray him as a man who lost control in these events. It was argued that the first murder was simply a tragic accident and the second one was just an effect of Christian's horrible past. His lawyers also pointed out that, out of all the women whom Christian met in person (and they were plenty), he had only murdered these two and all the others were completely fine. Christian does not want to be categorized as a serial killer for killing these two women whom he met on dating sites. The court declined his insanity appeal and he was seen as fit for trial. He received a sentence of life imprisonment on April 1, 2009.

Chapter 5: Thomas Montgomery

By now, the dangers of chatting online with strangers should be clear. The story of Thomas Montgomery has an unusual twist to it with a tragic ending.

In 2005, Thomas Montgomery, a forty-six-year-old married father of two living in Buffalo, New York, became consumed with frequenting online chat rooms. He particularly enjoyed a teen-only chat room hosted by the online gaming site Pogo.com. Using the name 'MarineSniper,' Tom pretended to be an eighteen-year-old version of himself, Tommy. He described himself as six-feet-tall, 180 pounds, with red hair and a large muscular build. He claimed he was a black belt in karate and a Marine on the verge of deployment to Iraq. It was in this chat room he met 'Talhotblond,' a seventeen-year-old high school senior named Jessi, who was living in West Virginia.

The two instantly hit it off in the chat room and it wasn't long before they became friends on MySpace and used Yahoo to instant message each other. They even exchanged phone numbers and began speaking over the phone and texting one another. Tom shared a photo of himself wearing a military uniform taken years prior during his six-year stint in the Marines. Jessi also shared photos of her own, some of them rather provocative. In quick time, the conversations between the two turned serious. They told each other that they were in love and neither of them had ever felt this way before.

Tom knew he was in over his head, but he later admitted that talking to Jessi every day was almost like an addiction. He couldn't quit her, no matter how hard he tried. He later claimed to be fully aware of his ridiculous obsession with a girl he could never be with, but he continued with the relationship. On Christmas day in 2005, Tom asked Jessi to marry him, and she accepted.

Finally, in March of 2006, the truth came out. Jessi messaged Tom when one of his daughters happened to be using his computer. Alarmed, his daughter showed her mother, Cindy. It wasn't long before Cindy intercepted one of Jessi's packages to her

36

husband and learned the truth. Searching the house, she uncovered a secret stash of letters, photos, and gifts from Jessi, including a small collection of her panties. Infuriated, Cindy mailed a letter to the return address on the package with a photo of her family, letting Jessi know the eighteen-year-old 'Tommy' she had been sending love letters to was a married forty-six-year-old man with two daughters nearly her age—twelve and fourteen. The jig was up. Tom moved into the basement of the family's Buffalo home when Cindy suggested they separate.

At first, Jessi was in denial. She went through Tom's list of friends on Pogo.com to confirm the truth. She contacted an individual who went by the screen name 'Beefcake,' Tom's twenty-two-year-old colleague named Brian Barrett. He was a young athletic man going to Buffalo State College part time and working at the Dynabrade power tool plant, hoping to one day become an industrial arts teacher. Brian confirmed the news to Jessi: Tom was indeed a married older man. Jessi texted Tom to tell him they were finished, admonishing him for swindling her. She was furious. Tom was crushed.

One would think that Jessi would learn her lesson after falling so hard for someone she didn't know at all. But as time went on, Jessi and Brian began to talk more and more and developed a relationship of their own. The two even began to flaunt their online relationship in front of Tom in the very same chat rooms he had first met Jessi. When Tom expressed his jealousy and anger towards the new couple, the two began exposing him in every chat room he entered, letting everyone know that he was nearly three times the age he claimed to be and that he was a married man. They called him a child predator and shamed him in front of others in the chat rooms.

But as time went on, Jessi also seemed to be playing Tom for a fool. The two never really stopped talking and even found themselves flirting with each other on occasion. It was almost as if Jessi couldn't let go of the image of Tommy she had formed in her head. And even after all the contention between the two when the truth had came out, he still couldn't stop chatting with her.

Tension between the two men at work grew thicker with each passing month. Some of their colleagues were aware of the odd love triangle and the contempt the two had for each other. Tom made verbal threats toward Brian. He began working out and his demeanor became dark and intense. Coworkers began to shy away from him, fearing what he might do.

Then one Friday night in September, Brian gathered up his things to leave work around 10:00. He walked out into the parking lot and got into his truck. Before he could even put the key in the ignition, gunfire rang out. He was shot three times at close range in the arm and neck and died nearly instantly in what authorities later described as a "sniper attack." His body remained in his truck for two days until someone found him on Monday morning.

Police canvassed the neighborhood to interview potential witnesses. They learned that locals had seen a man walking around the area that Friday night wearing camouflage and a ski mask. They also found a discarded peach pit on the ground near Brian's truck, which they bagged and saved as potential evidence. Learning of the online love triangle, police feared Tom might have been headed to Jessi's house in West Virginia. They sent a team of police to her house to make sure she was safe. A forty-five-year-old woman named Mary Shieler greeted them at the door. At first Mary told them her daughter Jessi was not home, but when she learned why they were there, she became visibly upset. Eventually she came clean with police and admitted that she was the one who had been communicating with Tom and Brian for the last year as 'Tallhotblond.' She had sent them both racy photos of her seventeen-year-old daughter, who was actually named Jessi.

On September 18, just three days after Brian's murder, police brought Tom in for questioning. They also searched his home, his car, and his cell phone and computer. On his computer, they uncovered a year and a half's evidence of chat records between Tom and 'Jessi,' as well as numerous threats Tom made to Brian online. They also located an owner's manual for a .38 military grade rifle, similar to the one that had killed Brian. Tom told them he had always wanted that type of gun, but just hadn't bought one yet. But then investigators found a photograph of his gun cabinet, displaying a .38 military grade rifle. Eventually, investigators were able to pin Tom to the murder using DNA from the discarded peach pit left at the scene and the photograph of his gun cabinet containing the type of rifle used in the crime.

Tom was officially arrested on November 27, 2006. He pleaded not guilty to second-degree murder. In August 2007, he took a deal with prosecutors and pleaded guilty to first-degree manslaughter, earning him a minimum of twenty years in prison. His wife divorced him.

Police also wanted to charge Mary with a crime, but they were unable to actually pin anything on her. Technically, she hadn't done anything illegal. Mary's husband also divorced her and her daughter Jessi moved away from the home, unable to forgive her mother for what she had done. Erie County Sheriff's Lt. Ron Kenyon spoke out about the case in an effort to warn the public about the dangers of connecting with people online. "When you're on the Internet talking, you haven't got a clue who that is on the other end," he said. "You don't have a clue."

Chapter 6: David Russell

As one of the most widely used social networks, Facebook has connected so many people. Old friends were able to find each other and distant families were able to meet again online. Facebook also offers the possibility for strangers to meet and become friends. However, the process of meeting someone new online can be very dangerous, and even deadly.

David Russell was a British man who worked at a McDonald's restaurant. For nineteen years, David led a flawless life. He was a good guy and a hard worker. However, this would all change when David turned twenty.

In 2010, David met nineteen-year-old Maricar Benedicto through Facebook. They chatted for a while. David posed as Oliver Sykes, the tattooed lead singer of the popular metal band called 'Bring Me The Horizon' and Maricar used the pseudonym Ruby Townsend. They also used Skype to chat. Maricar truly believed that David was indeed Oliver Sykes and decided to travel from the U.S. to the UK just to meet him. She had no way of knowing that she was going to meet a potential killer.

Maricar arrived in April of 2011. The night before her arrival, David surfed the internet searching for ways to kill someone with his bare hands, how to cut skin with a knife, and the best knife that he could use to kill. David met Maricar at the railway station and then took her to a forest not very far away.

David claimed that the place he was taking her to held some of his most special childhood memories. After they arrived in a secluded area, David asked Maricar to sit on a tree trunk. After that, he blindfolded her, claiming that he had a surprise to give her. Maricar completely trusted him and she let him blindfold her, and even complied when he asked her to put her arms up with her palms facing up and tilt her head back.

Maricar could not see anything, but she suddenly felt something sharp on her neck. She could feel her neck was being sliced open. While he was slitting Maricar's throat,

David screamed, "Why won't you die? You've ruined my life. It's all your fault." Maricar jumped up and when she did so, the blindfold that she had on her eyes fell off. She tried to run for her life, but David went after her. He stabbed her in her back three times. David then used a log to hit her in the face and head repeatedly. He did not stop until Maricar informed him that she had given his name and his address to the immigration officials when she arrived in the UK. After hearing this, David ran back to his home and is suspected of taking an overdose of medication. He left Maricar in the woods, fighting for her life. She barely managed to make her way to a house nearby where she was able to get help.

It was a miracle that Maricar had survived the attack. David was arrested and charged for kidnapping and attempted murder. The defense claimed that David suffered from borderline autism. They argued this was David's first offense and that he was simply a "troubled young man." However, on October 5, 2011, the Northampton Crown Court sentenced David to life in prison. He will not be up for parole for at least seventeen and a half years.

Commenting on the tragedy, Oliver Sykes, whose identity David used to lure the girl, said that he was very unsettled by the news; although people had used his identity before as a joke or to pull pranks, something which made him feel uncomfortable, this particular incident was terrifying. Oliver wished a good recovery for Maricar and directed people to the Carly Ryan Foundation, which raises awareness of the dangers of using the social networking sites and talking with strangers. In 2006, fifteen-year-old Carly Ryan was murdered by a fifty-year-old man posing online as an eighteen-year-old musician from Melbourne, Australia. The killer was caught and sentenced to life in prison without the possibility of parole for twenty-nine years. Ultimately though, Oliver hoped that people would be more careful in meeting strangers online.

Chapter 7: Robert Frederick Glass

Limitless information can be accessed with just a few clicks on the internet. Unfortunately, social media has also opened the door to unleashing many sick fantasies. An occurrence recognized by psychologists as the 'Mardi Gras phenomenon' (when someone assuming various personalities believes they can freely speak and act without consequences), has become a common occurrence online. People feel the internet allows them to express their fantasies anonymously and freely. One dark fantasy that Sharon Rina Lopatka had was to be tortured to death. By making her fantasy known through the internet, her wish became true.

Robert 'Bobby' Frederick Glass was a computer analyst working for the government of Catawba County, North Carolina. Forty-five-year-old Robert was a hard worker. As part of his responsibilities, he programmed the tax rolls and monitored the amount of gas consumed by the county vehicles. For nearly sixteen years, he worked for the government.

Robert was married and had three children: two daughters (ages ten and seven), and one son (age six). According to his wife Sherri, Robert was very interested in computers, to the point that he became more interested in computers than their marriage. Sherri noticed that Robert would spend a lot of time on his computer. Later, she discovered that Robert had been exchanging emails with other people using his online names 'Toyman' and 'Slowhand.' The emails were disturbing and violent. However, overall, Sherri described her husband as a good man who worked hard. His other side, he kept well hidden. In May of 1996, however, Robert and Sherri separated and she took custody of their children.

Sharon Rina Lopatka was born on September 20, 1961. Her active Orthodox Jewish parents raised her and her three younger sisters in the suburbs of Baltimore, Maryland. Sharon's classmates saw her as a normal girl who engaged in sports and participated in the school choir. In 1991, she married a Catholic man named Victor and moved into his home in Hampstead, Maryland. The marriage was her way of rebelling against her parents since they did not approve of their relationship.

Sharon soon started working from home. She earned money through the internet by rewriting ads, performing psychic readings, and selling pornographic videos. She had dangerous sexual fantasies and searched for someone willing to fulfill them. Sharon often logged into hard-core sexual chat rooms to chat anonymously with people interested in things like necrophilia, bondage, and sadomasochism.

Sharon was fascinated with the idea of torture until death. Over several months, she posted messages expressing her desire to be tortured to death. She received many responses, but none of the people writing her back were serious enough to actually go through with it. That is, until Sharon met Robert. The two met online through one of the chat rooms they both frequented. On paper, they were perfect for one another. Robert liked inflicting pain and Sharon wanted to be tortured. Sharon sent Robert an email

49

expressing her desire to be bound and then strangled when she was close to orgasm. When she asked him to fulfill this fantasy of hers, Robert accepted. Over the next few months, they continued to exchange emails and they finally decided to meet.

On October 13, 1996, Sharon told her husband that she was visiting a friend in Georgia. Instead, she took the morning train to North Carolina to meet Robert. He was waiting for her as she arrived and they drove together to his trailer home, some eighty miles away from the train station. Later, Sharon's husband found a note that she left for him, explaining that she was not coming back and asked him not to look for the person who killed her.

Victor immediately reported his wife missing. The police started an investigation and were able to link her to Robert by retrieving the emails exchanged between the two. They staked out Robert's trailer for a few days, hoping to catch a glimpse of Sharon who might still be alive, but there was no sign of her. On October 25, after obtaining a search warrant, the police raided the trailer while Robert was at work. The outside and inside of the trailer was filled with dirt and garbage. The police were able to locate some of Sharon's belongings in the trailer, as well as some other items of interest, including drugs, bondage items, a pistol, child pornography, and computer disks. But Sharon was nowhere to be found.

While searching the property, an officer wandered to an area seventy-five feet away from the trailer where he noticed the soil seemed freshly dug. He began digging and located Sharon's remains buried two and a half feet underground. Robert was arrested at his work the same day. He was interviewed and presented with the evidence found. Robert told the police that he and Sharon were simply fulfilling their sexual fantasies. She was willing, and he never made her do anything. During their intercourse, and at her request, Robert strangled Sharon. However, he claimed that her death was accidental.

The medical examiner reported that Sharon died of strangulation. There was some evidence of sexual torture, but ultimately the results were inconclusive. Sharon's death was considered to be deliberate, since she only met with Robert because he agreed to kill her. And because Robert had sent Sharon many emails containing details of how he wanted to kill her, the prosecution could argue that the murder was premeditated.

Robert was charged with first-degree murder. He was kept in the county jail. The charge was eventually reduced to voluntary manslaughter. On January 27, 1997, Robert pleaded guilty to this charge and to six counts of second-degree sexual exploitation of a minor for the child pornography found in his trailer. He received a sentence of thirty-six to fifty-three months for the first charge and twenty-one to twenty-six months for the second. Robert served his sentence at the Avery-Mitchell Correctional Institution in North Carolina. On February 20, 2002, just two weeks before his release, Robert died from a heart attack. This case was the first in which the police had zeroed in on a suspect relying only on evidence from emails.

Chapter 8: John Edward Robinson

With all the technological advancement and the extended use of the internet, it has become easier to reach out to friends and family all over the world. However, it has also become easier to meet strangers, near and far, and share interests or even dark desires. With the option to stay anonymous online, killers have been able to find their prey. "The internet's first serial killer," as he is referred to sometimes, was John Edward Robinson.

John Edward Robinson was born on December 27, 1943. John did not become a killer overnight. It is possible that his behavior was influenced at an early age by his disciplinary mother and alcoholic father. At age thirteen, he joined the Eagle Scouts and then enrolled in a private school for boys aspiring to be clerics. He dropped out after just a year. His early crimes included embezzlement, kidnapping, and forgery. He was first arrested in Kansas in 1969 for embezzlement, but he only received three years of probation, which he violated by moving to Chicago. In 1977, through lies and forgery, he was able to get himself elected onto the board of a charitable organization, forge letters to and from various authority figures to praise him, and name himself the organization's Man of the Year, where he organized a luncheon in his honor. On the surface, John was a nice man, a loving husband and father, and a good civilian. However, truly he was totally the opposite. He was also engaged in BDSM (bondage, discipline, sadistic, and masochistic behaviors).

John is known to have killed eight women, four of which he met through the internet. The actual number of his victims is unknown, but it can be established through the known victims that at least half of them were lured via the internet. No details of how he treated his victims were ever revealed, but he most likely killed them with one or two blows to the head using a blunt object, probably a hammer.

In 1984, John hired nineteen-year-old Paula Godfrey as a sales agent for one of his 'companies.' After telling her family and friends that she was going away for training, Paula disappeared. Her parents reported her missing to the police. John was questioned but he denied that he knew anything of Paula's whereabouts. Some days later, Paula's parents got a letter with her signature to assure them that she was fine but didn't wish to see them anymore.

In a strange twist to the story, John's brother and sister-in-law had been trying to adopt for years. One year before Paula's disappearance, in 1983, John convinced his brother that he would help him because he knew an attorney who handled private adoptions. For the next two years, John looked for a single mother with a young child. He was using the name John Osborne when he met nineteen-year-old Lisa Stasi and her four-month-old daughter Tiffany in Kansas in 1985. He convinced Lisa that he could give her a job and apartment in Chicago, and see that her baby be put in daycare. John also asked Lisa to sign some blank papers. At the same time, he informed his brother that he had found an infant up for adoption whose mother had committed suicide. He charged his brother \$5,500 (this is the actual amount paid: \$2,500 up front and then \$3,000 later) for the 'attorney fees' and brought baby Tiffany to his brother and his wife. Lisa disappeared without a trace.

In June 1987, John killed twenty-seven-year-old Catherine Clampitt after 'hiring' her and promising her a job with travel. Her remains were never discovered.

During a fraud conviction in 1993, he met a forty-nine-year-old librarian, Beverly Bonner, in a Missouri prison. After his release, he convinced her to leave her husband and come work for him in Kansas. He also arranged for her alimony checks to be forwarded to a post office box in Kansas, and then he killed her.

Between 1993 and 1994, John started using the internet to meet his next victims. He used the name 'Slavemaster' as his online screen name and started looking for a submissive sex partner. Bit by bit, he became known in BDSM chat rooms. His first victim he met online was forty-five-year-old Sheila Faith. She had a fifteen-year-old daughter named Debbie with cerebral palsy who was bound to a wheelchair. He promised to give Sheila a job and put Debbie in therapy. Upon moving to Kansas City, Missouri in 1994, Sheila and her daughter disappeared. John intercepted and cashed in Debbie's disability checks for the next seven years.

In 1999, he met twenty-one-year-old Polish immigrant Izabela Lewicka online. John, while still married, paid for a legal marriage certificate to wed Izabela, which he never collected. He also convinced Izabela to sign a 115-item 'slave contract' (a document stating she was giving him full control over her life, including her bank accounts). In the summer of the same year, Izabela disappeared.

John's last victim was a twenty-eight-year-old licensed nurse named Suzette Trouten. In 2000, John convinced her to move to Kansas so that they could travel together. Suzette disappeared without a trace soon after that.

The end for this merciless and greedy killer was getting closer. John was getting sloppy in covering up his tracks. He wrote letters signed by Suzette to her mother, claiming that they were having fun traveling to many places, but all the envelopes were postmarked from Kansas City. Also, they were written perfectly, something that Suzette wouldn't do. In addition, John's name was showing up in many missing person cases in both Kansas and Missouri. Finally, in the month of June 2000, the police were able to arrest John and obtain a search warrant for his farm in Kansas after one woman accused him of assault and another of theft. On the property, the police found the remains of Suzette Trouten and Izabela Lewicka in large barrels filled with chemicals. In Missouri, where John rented two storage units, barrels containing the remains of Beverly Bonner, Debbie Faith, and Sheila Faith were also found. In Kansas, he received the death penalty along with a sentence of life imprisonment for the murder of Lisa Stasi. In Missouri, after negotiations, John pleaded guilty and received life imprisonment without parole. Currently, John is on death row in Kansas, waiting to be the first person to be executed by lethal injection there.

Chapter 9: Ann Marie Linscott

The free Internet posting board, Craigslist, is used in over seventy different countries. Millions of ads are posted each year for people looking to sell things or searching for specific services. Occasionally though, one might find an odd posting on the site, perhaps one of the strangest ads was one looking for a hit man!

The online resume of Ann Marie Linscott has her listed in the 1970s as an assistant manager for the United Virginia Bank. From 1979 to 1982, she served in the U.S. Coast Guard in Alexandria, Virginia. It is stated that she earned an associate's degree from Ferris State College in 1986.

The next years of Ann Marie's life are largely unknown. However, in 1996, her name comes up in the records of Kent County Circuit Court. That year, Ann Marie filed a lawsuit against the Keebler Company, its union, and a couple of the company's employees. A restraining order was issued against one of the employees who in return had also taken a restraining order against her under the reason of unwanted sexual advances. The case was later moved to the federal court but was dismissed after a few court appearances, eight months later.

Some years later, in 2001, Ann Marie began working as a massage therapist, according to her resume. She worked for the Hospice of Grand Rapids and she met clients at the Riverview Athletic Club. However, no record of her employment was ever found there. One manager at the Riverview named Laurie Jordan stated that Ann Marie did not work there but she was given some space for her business as a massage therapist at the club in exchange for a percentage of her fee; few people used the massage services, and Ann Marie was only there three or four times each month.

At some point in time, Linscott had changed her name legally to Ann Marie, and had this name listed on her driving license. She was married to John Linscott, and had two children with him.

Around the year 2004 or 2005, Ann Marie took an online college course. She met a married man taking the same course and developed an online relationship with him. The two developed an intimate and deep relationship with each other online. They finally met in person when he traveled to Reno, Nevada where he was attending a conference in July of 2005. They spent two days together and had sexual relations. In May 2007, Ann Marie visited the man in Butte County, a place near his home. After that, they stayed in touch using telephone calls and sending emails. Ann Marie also expressed her desire to move to Butte County.

In April 2007, the man's wife found an intact Molotov cocktail in her bedroom connected to a fuse that had not exploded. Around November 2007, Ann Marie posted an ad on Craigslist searching for someone for a freelance job. She only revealed what she was actually looking for to those who emailed her in search for additional information. Three different people responded to the ad wanting to know more about the job, thinking it would be some sort of freelance writing job. However, as they communicated, Ann Marie made it clear that the job was about eradicating a woman who lived in Oroville, Butte County, California. When asked what exactly she meant by that, she replied and said "Duh, well, have her killed." She wanted to kill her lover's wife. She gave further information about the woman, such as her work and home address, and also gave a description and the age of the intended victim. For the job, she offered $5,000. She was determined to get rid of that woman.

The people who communicated with Ann Marie about the job, whom she called the "silent assassins," reported her to the law enforcement authorities in California. It wasn't long before the FBI was involved and Ann Marie was arrested at her home in Grand Rapids, Michigan (near Summit Avenue NE and 14 Mile Road) in January 2008. The man and his wife were also identified by the investigators, but their identity was not released to the public. The woman is only known in police reports by her initials C.Z. The man cooperated with the police, as he was also being investigated to determine if he was involved with this plan. He acknowledged his previous involvement with Ann Marie in past years.

The intended victim had to leave her family and her career in order for her to be hospitalized because of the stress, but she and her husband are working on a way to save their marriage. Ann Marie was charged with a murder for hire plot.

It was discovered that Ann Marie had a long history of getting too attached to another person (such might have also been the case with the employee from the Keebler Company). In the summer of 2008, while she was locked up, she wrote a love letter to the sheriff's deputy in the Newaygo County Jail after she was transferred to the Montcalm County Jail. She wrote, "I wish you'd send me a card with a little note letting me know you're thinking of me and missing me. I need something to hang onto! ... I think of you often every day."

In the 1997 case, her co-worker was obliged to file a personal protection order after she started stalking him.

Although the charges were initially filed in the Eastern District of California, Ann

Marie was able to plead guilty in the Western District of Michigan, her home state. Her lawyer claimed that she suffered from a borderline personality disorder and that she needed help with her mental illness. On February 4, 2009, the Honorable Janet T. Neff, U.S. District Court Judge sentenced Ann Marie Linscott to 151 months in prison (approximately twelve and a half years). In her ruling, she stated she believed that Ann Marie did not fully understand what she had done and showed no regret for her actions.

Chapter 10: Brian Horn

So many of the cases highlighted in this book seem to deal with people posing as others online. The case of Brian Horn may be one of the most difficult ones to read, as his victim was just twelve years old.

In 2010, thirty-four-year-old Brian Douglas Horn was a twice convicted sex offender, a cab driver, and a soon to be child killer. His prior sex offenses included two separate incidents of taking a young girl to his car, where he allegedly fondled and raped at least one of them. In 1998, he was arrested and charged with indecency with a juvenile and contributing to the delinquency of a juvenile.

From the start of his early life, Brian was an incredibly active and hyper infant. His mother claimed he was walking at five months and running at nine months. He would also stand in his crib and shake it violently—so much so that she took him to see a doctor. He was prescribed a drug called Thorazine, often used to treat severe behavioral disorders. When the drug made him nearly catatonic, his mother refused to give it to him any longer. In his later childhood, Brian was diagnosed with Attention Deficit Hyperactivity Disorder (ADHD) and she had great difficulty disciplining him. She claimed they were nearly evicted from their home because Brian liked to set paper airplanes on fire and send them coasting out the windows. He also created dangerous makeshift flamethrowers using a lighter and a can of hairspray.

Brian's parents were also arrested at one point for selling drugs out of their own home. The two had a contentious marriage, and separated several times before finally divorcing. In addition to the two sex-related offenses on Brian's record, he managed to rack up twelve other arrests in his adolescent and adult years.

In March of 2010, he convinced twelve-year-old Justin Bloxom that he was a fifteen-year-old girl named 'Amanda' who wanted to meet up with him for sex. The two met online through a social networking site and began to exchange sexually explicit text messages and photos. At one point, after Brian sent him a sexually provocative photo, Justin replied back, "you gotta remember, I'm only 12."

On March 29, 2010, Justin's mother dropped him off at a friend's house on Douglas Lane in Stonewall, Louisiana. His friend saw him texting someone during the night, and when he woke up in the morning, Justin was gone.

Phone records indicate that the night of his disappearance, Brian texted the young boy as Amanda, telling him 'she' would send a cab to pick him up so the two could meet and have sex. Unfortunately, Justin fell for the ruse and snuck out of his friend's house to rendezvous with the fictitious girl. Brian Horn picked Justin up in his taxicab on a nearby road, pretending to be the driver sent by 'Amanda.' Less than two hours later, Justin was dead and Brian had dumped his body in the woods. The manner of his death was later listed as asphyxiation.

Around 6:30 that morning, police had stopped Brian in the area where Justin's body would later be found. He told them he had locked his keys out of his cab and was waiting for a ride. They believed him and left him to his business. They had no idea Brian had just dumped a murdered child's body nearby. Once Justin was reported missing four hours later, however, they went back to the area to search for him.

Justin's body was found soon after in a marshy ditch in a wooded area near Highway 171 in Louisiana, near where police recalled seeing Brian's taxicab just hours before. Further searching of the wooded area turned up Brian's car keys and his cell phone charger. They immediately put out word they were looking for the twice-convicted sex offender. They didn't have to look long. Brian turned himself in soon after.

He was initially charged with second-degree murder, but the charges were increased as police uncovered the text messages the two had exchanged that night. He went to trial in 2014 officially charged with first-degree murder.

In a somewhat surprising turn of events, Brian's defense team did not call any witnesses, nor did they try to make a case for their defendant. During opening statements, his lawyers claimed the death had been an accident and his intent on luring the young boy into his cab was because he was a swinger and he wanted the child to have sex with his wife and girlfriend.

It took the jury just forty-five minutes to convict Brian Horn of first-degree murder. In April of 2014, the jury recommended he be given the death penalty. After the trial, all twelve jurors and the three alternates reached out to Justin's mother and asked if they could visit the Justin Bloxom Memorial Garden, a park set up in Justin's name after his murder. Together, they traveled to the garden and hugged his mother, ending the day holding hands and reciting a prayer for the twelve-year-old.

Following Justin's death, his family and friends formed the Justin Bloxom Alliance for Innocence, a private, non-profit organization aimed at spreading the word about the dangers children face in this era using the internet, social media sites, and cell phones. In addition, a number of bills have been passed in Louisiana and surrounding states, dubbed as "Justin's Law," that place stricter employment regulations on violent sex offenders to keep them away from children, as well as tougher penalties for repeat sex offenders.

Chapter 11: Anthony Powell

The internet has become a place where anyone can express his or her opinion about something. People can post whatever they want, making their voices heard. Some use Facebook or Twitter to express how they feel, and others post videos on YouTube for millions of people to see. Among these videos are people showing off their talents and passions, yet still others use the site to expose their hatred.

Anthony Powell was a twenty-eight-year-old Christian student at Henry Ford Community College. His parents were Sam Powell, a retired Detroit police officer, and Doris Powell, a registered nurse. He had suffered from chronic depression since his childhood and did not like to take medication, according to his mother. His parents had tried to help him, but they could not do any more than they had already done. Anthony's jobs varied, from working at a grocery store to restaurants.

Anthony was ambitious. He wanted to

work in the movie industry as a director or an actor. Among the classes he took in college was a theatre class, which he shared with Asia McGowan, who reportedly was an atheist. Asia was a special and extremely talented woman. She had a passion for dancing and acting. She was set to become a famous dancer and actress. Everyone admired Asia. Soon, Anthony developed feelings of love towards her and attempted to strike up a relationship with her. There is some speculation that the two were secretly dating, but Asia's friends and family have denied there is any truth behind those rumors.

Anthony Powell may have seemed normal if you met him in person, but online he was something else, and it was apparent that he was unbalanced. On YouTube, he posted many videos under the name 'Tony48219,' making statements against atheists and black women. In his videos, he would describe black women as being promiscuous. He went as far as posting one video with the title "Black Women Don't Deserve Respect." He also attacked atheists in his videos, calling them "stupid," being "the fallen angles of the devil," and as "not human," but instead "filthy animals." He clearly had a massive hatred toward atheists and their beliefs. He ranted about the theory of evolution and couldn't understand how anyone could believe in it. He also described evolution as a comedy, and would frantically laugh after. As a pro-creationist, Anthony was obsessed with another YouTube creationist, 'VenomFangX,' who created many videos about religion, Christianity, and God.

Asia also had an account on YouTube in which she posted various videos of herself, sometimes dancing. Anthony became obsessed with her and started stalking her using YouTube and Facebook (apparently they were friends on Facebook), while still posting his own videos. Some online users were alarmed by the types of videos that Anthony posted and tried to help him. In one video, he stated that he was going to kill himself because there was no point in living anymore but he was still scared to do it. One user living in Virginia with the online nickname 'Infamoustrag' found the videos so disturbing, he reported Anthony to the police on March 25, 2009. On April 2, 2009, 'Infamoustrag' received a reply from Chief James Barren's office thanking him for contacting them. The person left a name and a contact number for 'Infamoustrag' to contact them back. 'Infamoustrag' was able to make a link between Anthony's talk about suicide and him being upset over a girl. He tried to warn the Detroit Police about a possible suicide, but did not think that there would also be a murder committed by Anthony before his suicide. Another YouTube poster going by the online nickname 'DC Coop,' twenty-four-year-old Don Cooper from Atlanta, told Anthony that he should get help after he saw the video in which Anthony said that he wanted to kill himself.

On Good Friday, April 10, 2009, Anthony took a shotgun with him to the Mackenzie Fine Arts Center. At 12:30 p.m. that day, police were called in with a report of an assault. As soon as police arrived on the scene, they heard gunshots. The college went into lockdown so that the police would make sure that there were no other threats and a gunman was not still at large. They soon discovered the bodies of Anthony and Asia in one of the classrooms. Apparently, Anthony used the shotgun to murder Asia and then kill himself.

Although the motives behind this murder may look religious, investigators believe it was caused by a combination of depression, hatred, and fanaticism. Anthony's parents were shocked to learn their son could do something like this. They did not know where he could have gotten the gun since they did not keep any guns at home. His mother knew that he suffered from depression and he had a history of mental illness, and that he might kill himself. She had tried to offer him help, but she did not expect that he would take someone else's life in the process. Anthony's parents offered their condolences to Asia's parents and they said that they were very sorry for the actions of their son. Asia's father, Turahn McGowan, was shocked from the videos that Anthony had posted and wished that someone could have helped Anthony before he took the life of his daughter, especially since the police had been warned about him before.

75

The death of Asia McGowan should be a wakeup call to stop intolerance towards other people's beliefs and opinions, especially in a time where anyone can share anything with the entire world.

Chapter 12: David Heiss

Some people live their entire lives online. They become so engaged in this virtual life to the point that they can't recognize what is real and what is not. Generally, these people lack social skills and like to hide behind the online anonymity. Some even become a danger to others who are not careful about keeping their personal information a secret. When the line between reality and fantasy is shattered, there's no telling what could happen

David Heiss grew up living with his grandmother and his aunt in Dauborn in the west central region of Germany. His parents divorced when he was six years old. He rarely saw his mother, who worked as a nurse and lived with her daughter in Limburg, fifteen kilometers away from Dauborn, and he saw or talked with his father even less. For about two years, he lived in the family home. David was very close to his grandparents. He was devastated when his grandfather died, and when his grandmother fell ill, his sadness deepened.

David was a student at Limburg's Tilemannschule. The school had great facilities and a good reputation. He was a good student, excelling in German, politics, biology, mathematics, and Catholic religion. At age nineteen, he left school but despite his good grades, he was not able to get into a university because he could not afford the costs. Instead, he joined the military after school. However, he was injured and he soon dropped out. His mother noticed that after his experience in the military, he seemed distressed. She tried to make him see a psychologist, which he did only twice. Then, David got a job at a textile dye production company. He had to travel to Frankfurt daily, and he earned about £600 per month.

On his Facebook page, David listed Faust, the main character of a classic German legend, as his favorite character. The character was highly successful but dissatisfied with his life, so he had made a pact with the devil. Politically, on Facebook David listed himself as liberal, and as for his relationship status, he was single. Some of his favorite bands were Metallica, Queen, and the Foo Fighters; some of his favorite movies were Pulp Fiction and Star Wars; some of his favorite activities were football, chess, video gaming, and using the internet.

When he was not at his work, David was online, surfing the world of online games. He spent many hours in internet forums chatting with other people who had the same interests in gaming, especially strategy gaming. However, David felt a bit jealous of these people whom he chatted with online because many of them were able to attend college, unlike him.

Warcentral.com was a website managed by twenty-year-old Matthew Pyke and his twenty-year-old girlfriend, Joanna Witton. David spent much of his time chatting with other gamers on this Advance Wars fan website, which contained around 300 members. There, he used the nickname 'Eagle the Lightning,' where he could pretend he wasn't David, a man who could not afford to go to a university.

During that time, David became interested in Matthew's girlfriend, Joanna, who went by the online nickname 'Jojo.' At one point, he sent her a message declaring his love for her. It said,

"I love you Jojo more than anything else in my life. I shouldn't, but I can't help it, and to be honest, it's a great feeling. You are my first thought when I wake up and the last one when I go to sleep."

Although they had not yet met, David began stalking Joanna online, sending her messages, going through her Facebook profile, and checking her online diary. He kept doing so even though she never encouraged his behavior. By June 2008, David was able to get Matthew and Joanna's home address in Nottingham, and he traveled from Germany to England to pay them a visit twice, once in June and once in August.

David continued his obsessive behavior, despite Joanna's rejections. She advised him to seek professional help from a psychologist, and blocked him from the website. By September 17, 2008, Joanna had stopped all contact with David. He could not take it, so he decided to pay Matthew a deadly visit. On September 19, David flew to the United Kingdom one more time. He waited outside Matthew and Joanna's apartment until Joanna had left for work. Then he knocked on the door and as soon as Matthew opened the door, David attacked him. He stabbed Matthew eighty-six times, ultimately killing him. Joanna discovered Matthew's body later that day. David left the scene after trashing the apartment to make it look like a robbery attempt gone wrong, got rid of the knife somewhere along the way, and caught a flight back to his home in Germany within sixteen hours.

Before Matthew died, he tried to write the name of his killer using his blood, and he managed to write "DAV." On September 24, 2008, David was arrested at his home. David claimed that he was acting in self-defense. He claimed that Matthew had attacked him first with the knife. However, in May of 2009, David was sentenced to a life in prison. The judge, who described David's motive as "bizarre," ordered him to spend at least eighteen years in prison before he would be eligible for parole.

When Matthew's mother heard about her son's death, she could not believe it, especially because Matthew was not the type to get into a fight. His brother, Adam, later expressed how difficult it was to accept his brother's death, and talked about how great Matthew was. During the trial, when asked why she didn't block David earlier, Joanna replied that she was afraid that she would only escalate the situation, and when the defense asked what she meant by that, she tearfully replied, "Look what happened. I'm sorry, but look what happened."

The case received a lot of attention because of the way in which David had met Mathew and Joanna, how he became obsessed with Joanna, and how in the end he plotted to kill Matthew. It brought light to the amount of people who live their lives online believing their virtual lives and relationships are real and falsely believing that the digital age provides them with true anonymity.

Chapter 13: Lisa M. Montgomery

Lisa Marie Montgomery was born on February 27, 1968 in Melvern, Kansas. Her childhood was anything but happy. She later reported suffering physical and sexual abuse at the hands of her stepfather, whom her mother divorced when she was sixteen.

Lisa married her stepbrother, Carl Borman, in 1986, when she was just eighteen. According to Carl, Lisa loved the attention she got when she was pregnant. The couple had four children in less than four years. Lisa later claimed that Carl and her mother forced her to undergo a tubal fulguration (a process in which a woman's fallopian tubes are cauterized using an electromagnetic current, causing sterilization) to avoid having any more children. Over the next few years, Lisa pretended to be pregnant twice. Tired of her lies, Carl divorced her in 1993, but the couple married again in 1994. They finally broke up for good in 1998, when Lisa took the children and moved in with a man named Kevin Montgomery, who lived in

Melvern, Kansas. He had three children of his own and lived with his parents. The couple married in 2000.

During her marriage to Kevin, Lisa pretended to be pregnant several times, and each time she eventually claimed she had lost the baby due to miscarriage. During those times, she would wear maternity clothes and tell others about her approaching due date. Not knowing that Lisa had undergone sterilization, Kevin believed his wife was actually pregnant each time.

Meanwhile, Carl was busy battling Lisa in court for custody of his children. He knew she was still lying about becoming pregnant and told her he would make her admit her lies in open court, which he believed would give him an advantage in the custody battle. As the court date loomed, Lisa began scheming. She began watching videos online of home births and Cesarean section procedures.

On December 15, 2006, using the name 'Darlene Fischer,' Lisa contacted a woman named Bobbie Jo Stinnett in an online forum called 'Ratter Chatter,' where rat terrier breeders often posted about dog shows and puppies for sale. Lisa was a frequent poster to the forum, and in fact, she had met Bobbie Jo earlier that year at a dog show in April, right around the time Bobbie Jo had begun telling people in the forum she was pregnant and due in January. Lisa also began telling people she was pregnant again around the same time, claiming her due date was December 16. Bobbie Jo and her husband, Zebulon (Zeb) James Stinnett, were dog breeders. The two were high school sweethearts and this would be their first child. Bobbie Jo had also posted pictures on the website for her breeding business, Happy Haven Farms, indicating that she was pregnant. Posing as 'Darlene,' Lisa told Bobbie Jo that she wanted to buy one of her rat terrier puppies. Bobbie Jo gave her address to Darlene, who agreed to meet her the next day. Lisa then searched the internet for directions to Bobbie Jo's home and there is evidence she actually drove the 130 miles to Skidmore, Missouri that day as a 'dry run.' Bobbie Jo told her husband and her mother that she had a potential buyer for one of the puppies in their litter and she would be stopping by the next day.

On December 16, Lisa again drove the 130 miles to Bobbie Jo's home. Inside her jacket, she concealed a white cord and a sharp kitchen knife. Witnesses later recalled seeing a red Toyota Corolla parked in the driveway of the Stinnett residence. A gruesome and violent struggle took place inside the home that day, ending with Lisa fleeing the residence with Bobbie Jo's premature baby.

When Bobbie Jo's mother arrived at the home about an hour later, she found her pregnant daughter lying dead in a large pool of blood in the dining room. According to court documents, she called 911 in hysterics and told the operator that it looked like her daughter's stomach had "exploded or something."

Paramedics tried to revive Bobbie Jo, but it was clear that she had died at the scene. Crime scene analysts determined that she had been strangled from behind and her stomach had been sliced open laterally with a kitchen knife. The fetus had been pulled from her dead mother's body and her umbilical cord had been cut. Investigators also found strands of blondish-brown hair in Bobbie Jo's closed fist, indicating she had fought violently with her attacker.

Alarmed that this mother to be had been brutally murdered and her premature fetus had been cut from the womb, quick-thinking police issued an AMBER alert, along with the description of Lisa's car that had been parked in the driveway earlier. They had no idea if the baby had survived the attack, but the AMBER alert helped spread the word quickly.

Meanwhile, Lisa called her husband a short time later, claiming she had gone shopping out of town that day and had gone into labor. She told him that she had given birth to a healthy baby girl at a women's clinic in Topeka, Kansas. Miraculously, the baby had survived the brutal attack with little more than a cut over her eye. Lisa clamped the umbilical cord by herself and placed the infant in a car seat she had brought with her. Kevin and two of his older children met Lisa in Topeka and they all drove home.

The next day, Lisa and Kevin took the child, whom they named Abigail, out on the town. They went out for breakfast with the infant and showed her off to everyone they saw. Witnesses later described being alarmed that the couple had taken a one-day-old infant out around town.

Police made quick progress tracking down Lisa. They had a description of her car, thanks to neighbors who had remembered seeing it parked outside the Stinnett's home. Word in the Ratter Chatter forum about Bobbie Jo's horrific murder spread quickly and one of the members contacted police about something she remembered from the day before the murder: a meeting Bobbie Jo had arranged with a woman named Darlene Fischer. Police quickly tracked 'Darlene's' IP address to Lisa's home in Melvern, Kansas, where they spotted the same car described by witnesses, and Lisa with an infant.

On December 17, just one day after Bobbie Jo's murder, police knocked on Lisa and Kevin's front door. They told the couple they were investigating the murder of Bobbie Jo Stinnett and began to ask Lisa about her baby. At first, Lisa told the same story she had told her husband—that she had given birth at a women's clinic in Topeka, Kansas the day before. She then asked to speak to the officers in private. Outside of her husband's earshot, she told police that she had actually given birth at home and she had thrown the placenta in a nearby river. At this point, officers brought Lisa to the Sheriff's office, where she ultimately confessed to killing Bobbie Jo and cutting the infant from her womb.

The child was safely returned to Zeb Stinnett, who named her Victoria Jo. The pastor who had married the couple just one year earlier gave a eulogy at twenty-three-year-old Bobbie Jo's wake.

Lisa was charged with kidnapping Victoria Jo, resulting in the death of Bobbie Jo. Her defense team claimed insanity, asserting that Lisa suffered from various mental diseases such as depression, borderline personality disorder, post-traumatic stress disorder, and pseudocyesis, a clinical term describing a condition in which a woman believes she is pregnant when she is not. People with this condition may even experience symptoms of pregnancy, such as swelling of the abdomen, enlarged breasts, menstruation cessation, and even sensations of faux fetal movement. The defense did not try to deny that Lisa had killed Bobbie Jo; rather they tried to convince the jury that her mental state, along with the physical and mental abuse she had suffered from as a child, caused her to commit the crime in a delusional dissociative state.

The jury didn't buy it. Confronted with testimony from the state's expert witnesses, along with gruesome crime scene photos, and the 911 call from Bobbie Jo's mother, jurors found Lisa Montgomery guilty and later issued a death penalty verdict. Lisa's attorneys filed an appeal, trying to get their client off on a technicality. They claimed that Victoria Jo could not be considered a person until she was removed from her mother's womb, and since Bobbie Jo had died *before* Victoria Jo was removed, the charge of kidnapping resulting in death wasn't a possible scenario. A federal appeals court panel upheld the conviction in 2011. In 2012, the U.S. Supreme Court denied to hear the case.

Lisa currently sits on death row in Fort Worth, Texas, awaiting her execution.

Chapter 14: Edward Frank Manuel

Sharing personal information online is a somewhat new trend. People write about their interests and meet new people without ever actually knowing whom they might be talking to. It could be a man pretending to be a woman or a criminal pretending to be interested in the services offered in ads. Dangerous murderers are luring their victims through the internet on sites like Craigslist and chat room websites. Although it's been harder for the police to prevent these kinds of crimes, in the very few times in which a would-be-murder-victim is saved from a killer, it is considered a victory. This is what happened with the case of Edward Frank Manuel.

Edward was a fifty-five-year-old man living in Houston in 2003. He was married and worked as a technical communications consultant. He began frequenting suicide chat rooms, meeting people. There are reports that Edward had bragged to others in this particular chat room that he had helped suicidal people end their suffering. It was there he met an anonymous woman from Wisconsin who expressed her desire to die. She asked Edward for his help and he agreed to kill her.

Edward allegedly told the woman to sell all of her belongings and make the trip to Texas where the two would meet up at the Houston bus terminal. They agreed they would dig her grave together in a state park. Then Edward would strangle her during sex, place a yellow rose on her chest, and bury her where no one would find her.

On his way to the bus station, the police stopped Edward in his car. With him, they found yellow roses and what appeared to be a strangling device, but the police have never disclosed what that device really was. The would-be-victim who did show up and was waiting for Edward at the bus stop was actually playing a part in this planned police operation, but her identity remains unknown. It is unclear if she contacted the police after having second thoughts or if the entire operation was a plot to capture a potential murderer.

After Edward bonded out of jail for $10,000 and was waiting for his next court appearance in January 2003, the media nicknamed him the "Internet suicide chat room killer." He was facing a possible twenty years behind bars for an attempted capital murder charge.

You might find it odd that a man who did not actually commit murder or even attack this woman could be charged with attempted capital murder. Even if he did have yellow roses in his car, along with some sort of device that may have been used for strangling, did the police have probable cause to arrest him when he could have been meeting the woman out of curiosity?

His lawyers must have thought the same thing. They were able to arrange a plea bargain with the state of Texas. Edward pleaded guilty to attempted murder, and he was given just ten years of probation, which he completed in 2013, and no additional jail time.

The suicide chat room disappeared, but the postings appear somewhere else online. The woman's motives are unknown and it is still unclear if she was working for the police the entire time. What is clear is the fact that potential killers will look anywhere to find vulnerable victims, including places where people go to find comfort and feel safe.

Chapter 15: George Bernard Lamp, Jr.

In this new age of technology, finding things has never been easier. Whether a person is looking for a job, items to buy at lower cost, services... practically anything can be found with the help of the internet. However, the internet is also at the disposal of criminals who are able to find their victims with a just few clicks. One of the widely used sites for these kinds of services is Craigslist. As a result, we have seen a new type of killer dubbed by the media as 'Craigslist killers' and George Bernard Lamp, Jr. fits right into that category.

George Bernard Lamp, Jr. was born on December 21, 1957. Before he committed his first and only murder in March 2008, George was charged with kidnapping and an attempt to sexually assault a woman he met online in the fall of 2007. The woman was working as an escort (like his next unlucky victim). George was using the name Greg Lamp. They met on October 8, 2007 at a convenience store close to Troutman, North

Carolina. George drove her to Perth Road, where he attempted to rape her and then forced her to perform a sexual act. Then he tied her up, put her facedown in the backseat, and drove to the northbound rest area on Interstate 77, near Mooresville. As he was pulling her out of the car, she was able to break free and escape. George jumped back into his car and drove away. However, there was someone who witnessed what had happened. George was arrested, and after he pleaded guilty, he received a probationary sentence.

George used Craigslist to lure his next victim. On the February 10, 2008, he placed an ad under the category 'erotic services,' claiming he was searching for a woman to keep him company. He described himself as a "good looking white professional male." Unfortunately for fifty-two-year-old Bonnie Lou Irvine, she responded to the ad.

Apparently, George and Bonnie exchanged a number of emails in which he identified himself as Greg Lamp. She also directed him to other pictures of herself at other websites popular to men searching for prostitutes. Her friends and family last saw Bonnie when she left her home in Cornelius, North Carolina on February 28, 2008. George killed her and her body wasn't found until March 14.

On March 2, George placed another ad on Craigslist, this time looking for a mechanic. He said that he was having problems with the alarm system of his girlfriend's Volvo—it was going off and he wasn't able to get into the car (the car was actually Bonnie's). On March 13, George placed his last ad looking for a woman. Although Bonnie was last seen on February 28, her roommate did not report her missing until March 8.

On March 13, the FBI task force, along with the N.C. State Bureau of Investigation, stopped the 2001 Volvo George was driving at a Citgo Station near Exit 42 off Interstate 77. They had been looking for Bonnie's car and when they ran the license plate on the one George had been driving, they learned it belonged to a Ford Contour owned by Bernard Lamp. They were able to arrest George on charges he had violated his probation. The car contained evidence and blood, which led them to a house on Weathers Creek Road, in Troutman, North Carolina. In the backyard, the authorities found a shallow grave, which contained Bonnie's body.

On March 22, 2008, George was charged with one count of a first-degree murder and one count of a first degree kidnapping. He would wait six long years for his trial. In January 2014, the trial for the murder of Bonnie began. Jury selection started on January 13, and testimony began one week later, on January 20. The defense had one small victory when the kidnapping charges were dropped.

The medical examiner presented evidence George had strangled the victim. Although there were no scratches on her neck, she had injuries indicating she had been struck in the face several times and manually strangled. There were no ligature marks, which indicated her murderer gripped his hands tight around her throat as she tried to free herself. Bonnie was likely rendered unconscious in as few as ten seconds, but it took her several minutes to actually die.

Four professionals testified about the evidence found on women's clothing that was found in the garage of the house where Bonnie had been buried. Stephen Shawn, a hair and fiber expert, testified that a hair sample he examined was similar to Bonnie's but no definite conclusion about the test could be reached. Jennifer Ramirez, a nuclear DNA expert, and Megan Peterson, a serologist (the scientific study of plasma serum and other bodily fluids), both testified that the testing of the blood found on the clothing was positive, but the confirmation tests were negative or there wasn't enough evidence to be tested. Dr. Susan Croup, an expert in mitochondrial DNA, explained to the jury that the mitochondrial DNA inherited from the mother is not unique for each individual; there was not any item submitted for the test which had a positive match for Bonnie or George, however, they cannot be excluded. Among the tested items were two head hairs—one retrieved from the tape on the plastic bag that contained the victim's body and another retrieved from a black purse located in the trash can at the house of George's brother.

Moreover, the owner of the home where the body of the victim was found, Leslie Belkin, was a friend of George's. Neighbors testified about seeing him at the residence, burning things in the backyard where the corpse was discovered. In addition, neighbors also testified about seeing him driving a 2001 Volvo (the victim's car), and someone saw him take out something out of the trunk of the car. In total, thirty-eight witnesses testified and 270 pieces of evidence were presented.

George was found guilty of the first-degree murder of Bonnie Lou Irvine on February 5, 2014. The jury deliberated for just three hours and forty minutes before reaching a verdict at the Iredell County Superior Court. On February 19, the jury recommended the death penalty.

Chapter 16: Hiroshi Maeue

Suicide chat rooms are a popular way for those suffering from depression to find comfort with our people who are going through something similar. Unfortunately, as we have learned, those people can also become easy prey to the sick minds lurking online, searching for a victim. By sharing information about themselves and their situation, they may be unknowingly opening themselves up to a murderer.

Hiroshi Maeue was born in Japan on August 8, 1968. As a bright man in his twenties, Hiroshi attended the Kanazawa Institute of Technology. However, around 1988, he tried to strangle one of his male friends, which resulted in him dropping out of the institute. Later in 1995, Hiroshi was arrested after he attacked and attempted to strangle a work associate. The case was settled out of court, but Hiroshi was later fired from his job. Some years later, in 2001, he was arrested again for trying to strangle two women. This time, he was sentenced to spend one year in prison, with a three-year suspended sentence. A short time later, Hiroshi was released on good behavior. Not long after his release, in 2002, he was arrested once more for trying to strangle a boy in junior high school. He again received a sentence of twenty-two months in prison.

Hiroshi later claimed that, as a child, he read a mystery novel that affected him deeply and that was what triggered his later deadly crimes. He claimed to become sexually excited by killing people.

After he was released from prison in 2005, he began logging into online suicide chat rooms. It was there he was able to meet and lure his victims. He killed his first victim in February of 2005. Hiroshi had been emailing twenty-five-year-old Toyonaka resident Michiko Nagamoto for some time. Michiko was severely depressed. They made a pact to commit suicide together by sitting in a sealed car with a charcoal burner, peacefully dying from carbon monoxide poisoning. The two met up on February 19, 2005, in a car that Hiroshi had rented. After having a brief conversation, Hiroshi suffocated the woman using his bare hands. According to later testimony, he used his hands to hold her nose and mouth shut. On February 23, police found her body and were able to identify her using her fingerprints. Hiroshi had buried her corpse along a river in a mountainous area in Kawachinagano, Osaka Prefecture.

A couple of months later, in May 2005, Hiroshi lured out his second victim. Using the same method, he was able to murder a fourteen-year-old boy from Kobe. A month later, in June 2005, Hiroshi claimed another victim. He killed a twenty-one-year-old college student. Both of these bodies were abandoned in two separate areas in the mountains of southern Osaka Prefecture.

Meanwhile, investigators were trying to track down the killer. They were able to identify Hiroshi as the murder when they traced emails he had exchanged with his first victim, Michiko Nagamoto. They also looked into the car rental contract. Hiroshi was arrested on August 5, 2005 for the murder of Michiko. After his arrest, he confessed to have killed two other victims (the junior high boy and the college student). The police checked missing persons reports and were able to confirm his other victims.

It is believed that Hiroshi had posted on many other suicide websites. The reason behind his murders was sexual. He suffered from paraphilia and a psychosexual disorder and claimed he was not able to reach a sexual release and have sexual pleasure unless he could perform an act of strangulation. He enjoyed watching his victims suffocate in agony.

During his trial, the prosecutors went after the death penalty. They argued that Hiroshi would remain a threat because he would not be able to resist the sexual urges that made him commit the crimes in the first place. On March 28, 2007, the Osaka District Court sentenced Hiroshi to death. The judge talked about how Hiroshi's condition was untreatable, saying, "the crime was cruel, harsh and outrageous." When asked if he would commit these crimes again on the condition he was released, Hiroshi replied, "I have worries." The defense team tried to file an appeal, but on July 5, 2007, it was retracted. Hiroshi accepted his fate and was willing to pay for the crimes he committed. On July 28, 2009, Hiroshi was hanged in Osaka.

108

Chapter 17: John Katehis

John Katehis committed his first and only murder when he was just sixteen years old. And he found his victim through Craigslist.

John Katehis, an American student, was born in the year 1992. Not much is publicly known about his childhood and his early teenage years. However, it is noted that, as any other teenager, he used the internet and had many different accounts on various sites including a MySpace account and even an illegal XTube account (because this website is the equivalent YouTube for pornography and all users must be eighteen years of age to have an account, John was pretending to be eighteen at the time).

On his profiles, he wrote his age (but not on XTube) and where he lived in New York. He also stated his hobbies (riding bikes, hopping roofs, hanging out, listening to music on his iPod, and Parkour exercises), how he liked doing wild things and taking risks, and was open into having conversations with others. He also said that he was a LaVeyan

Satanist and a sadomasochist.

The road to murder was pretty easy for John. Looking to make easy and fast money, he responded to an ad on Craigslist on March 18, 2009. The ad was posted by George Weber, a forty-seven-year-old radio reporter working as a freelance anchor for ABC News Radio. George was advertising for a sexual erotic encounter, rough sex, and he was looking for someone to smother him. For $60, John agreed to meet George and bind his feet with some duct tape and smother him as a part of the act required. They agreed to meet on March 20, 2009.

That day, one of George's neighbors saw a young man, believed to be John, speaking on his cellphone outside the building in which George lived. Around 6:00 p.m., George invited John in. We only have John's account of what happened next that day.

According to John, once he was inside the apartment, George offered him cocaine. Everything was going according to the plan and John bound George's ankles, like he asked. After that, George pulled out a knife and attacked John. They wrestled and both struggled for the knife and suddenly the knife went through George's neck, piercing his jugular vein. John claimed when he pulled the knife out of George's neck, he cut his hand. He said it was his first time trying cocaine and he became extremely paranoid as everything happened so fast. Then, John changed his clothes, which were now stained with blood, and left the apartment. Around 9:13 p.m. someone spotted John on a northbound G train, bleeding from his hand. At the station, Emergency Medical Services met him and took him to Elmhurst Hospital Center. There, he was treated and released. John told the doctors that he received the cut on his left hand by a broken bottle. The body of the victim was not found until two days later in his apartment in Carroll Gardens, Brooklyn.

Police were able to identify John down through the emails he had exchanged with the victim after connecting on Craigslist. Although John had no criminal record, the police still suspected him. After the murder, John had gone to one of his friend's home, but the detectives were able to track him down with the help of John's father, who convinced his son to meet him at a bus depot in Middletown, New York on March 24, 2009. As John arrived at the depot, the police closed in on him.

Once John began talking, his story of self-defense was a bit hard to believe. First of all, the police couldn't find any traces of drugs in George's apartment. Secondly, according to the medical examiner, George wasn't stabbed just once; he was stabbed around fifty times in the neck, shoulders, hands, chest, and rear torso as well. The victim was left to bleed to death. Furthermore, the weapon used to stab George was never found. Finally, during the forty-minute confession he gave police, John sounded at ease, laughing every once in a while and eating a doughnut.

John claimed that he only stabbed the victim once and when he left the apartment after taking the $60 from his pocket, George was still moving. However, the prosecutor argued that the murder was not a result of an accident or a struggle and that George was no threat to John. On the other hand, the defense countered that the victim was indeed a sexual predator and stated that John had been "used by an older gentleman."

Although John committed the murder when he was sixteen years old, he was charged as an adult with second-degree murder. He was also charged with illegal possession of a weapon. After the jury wasn't able to reach a verdict, a second jury was formed and John was found guilty in November of 2011. On December 13, John was sentenced to twenty-five years to life, the maximum sentence.

Chapter 18: Peter Chapman

In 2009, online safety became a prominent theme in the UK media. In October of that year, a tragedy struck the Hall family. Their seventeen-year-old daughter, Ashleigh, was taken away from them after she had met a man on Facebook posing as a teenage boy. The case caused many to criticize Facebook for not providing a pedophile 'panic button,' like other social media sites in the UK that allows users who believe they are being targeted by a pedophile to directly connect to the Child Exploitation and Online Protection (CEOP) Centre's website. There, trained people help the individual deal with the situation they are facing and give them the opportunity to report the case to the police if necessary. Ashleigh's family believes if Facebook had signed up to implement the panic button, their daughter might still be alive today.

Peter Chapman was born in January 1977 in Darlington, County Durham, in the northeast region of England. He grew up in

Stockton with his grandparents. At the age of twenty-six, Peter moved to Liverpool. In 2007, he returned to County Durham, and then to Merseyside.

Way before all this moving around, Peter was charged with multiple sexual assaults. His long history of being investigated for sexual offenses began when he was just fifteen years old. At age nineteen, he was sent to spend seven years in prison after raping two prostitutes at knifepoint. Peter was released in 2001. He was supposed to be monitored by the police, but he somehow fell off their radar.

In 2003, Peter picked up a prostitute in the Liverpool's red light district, and they agreed on a £60 fee for sex. She was just twenty-six years old and a drug addict at that time. Peter took the woman to an apartment nearby, and once they were inside he told her to take off her clothes. When she demanded that he give her the money first, he attacked her. He placed duct tape on her mouth and also used it to tape her hands together. The woman begged him not to hurt her, but he held her down and raped her. The entire time, he held a twelve-inch-long knife and threatened to kill her if she refused to do what he said. After he was done, he apologized and told her that he did not mean to hurt her, but then raped her again. She was held captive for fifteen hours. After that, Peter forced the woman to get back into his car and he dropped her off close to the area where he had picked her up earlier. The woman reported what had happened to the police and gave them a description of the apartment where she had been taken. The investigators were able to use her description to locate Peter. He was charged with kidnapping and raping the woman.

Unfortunately, by the time the case finally went to trial, the woman could not face him. The case collapsed and Peter was allowed to walk out of the courtroom a free man. The woman expressed her regret later because, had she been brave enough, Peter wouldn't have been free to kill Ashleigh Hall.

After that, Peter stayed in Liverpool where he began a relationship with Dyanne Littler, a twenty-five-year-old mother. However, when Dyanne found out that Peter was on the public register of sex offenders, she ended her relationship with him.

Peter liked using the internet because it allowed him to stay somewhat anonymous. Using the social media, Peter was able to contact 2,981 girls between the ages of thirteen and thirty-one. More than 800 comments were posted on his Facebook page. He was a balding thirty-three-year-old man with bad teeth, but on Facebook he pretended to be a handsome teenager named Pete Cartwright. For his birthday, he used the same month and day, but he selected a year to look so much younger. It was through Facebook where he met seventeen-year-old Ashleigh Hall. That same day, 100 other girls accepted his friend request. He sent Ashleigh a picture of a bare chested boy, which he claimed to be of himself. On October 21, 2009, Ashleigh agreed to meet with him. He told her that his dad would pick her up on the day they picked. Before meeting with Ashleigh, Peter also tried to lure another girl who was fifteen years old, but he was unsuccessful.

October 25, 2009 was a Sunday. Ashleigh told her mother that she was going to her friend's house, but she was actually planning on meeting Peter. Peter headed to the place where they agreed to meet. He had two mobile phones; one was 'Pete's' and the other was 'Pete's Dad's.' He sent a message to Ashleigh pretending to be Pete's dad, asking if she doesn't mind him picking her up and how Pete can't wait to see her. She replied that she didn't mind and that she trusted Pete and his father.

Peter then used the second mobile to text her, pretending to be Pete. His message was: *"Me dad's on his way babe. he says excuse the state of him lol He's been at work lol he doesn't have to come in and meet your mum does he he'll be a mess probably....hope you are wearing some sexy underwear for me hehe x."* When he arrived, he sent another message pretending to be Pete telling her that his dad was there.

Ashleigh got into the car with Peter. He drove her to a secluded area in Thorpe Arches, Durham. Using duct tape, he wrapped her head, legs and arms. He then

119

made her perform a sex act before he raped her. Before he suffocated her, Peter made his poor victim get dressed. He then wrapped duct tape around her face and suffocated her. He dumped the body near a Little Chef restaurant in Sedgefield, County Durham. He knew if he let her live she would be able to tell police about his Facebook profile, his car, where he lived, and his mobile phone numbers. Letting her go alive was too risky for Peter.

Peter was on his way to meet with another woman when he decided to pass by the crime scene to make sure that the body of Ashleigh was not spotted. However, on his way there, a traffic cop became suspicious of him. He ran his license plate and found out that Peter was wanted for a motoring offense. The cop arrested Peter and brought him to the Middleborough police station. There, he confessed to the murder of Ashleigh Hall. He led the police to the junction of the A689 and A177 roads, and there they found the dressed corpse of Ashleigh. Since Peter was a registered sex offender, he was required to stay in Merseyside after he was released from prison but the police had failed to keep him on their radar. When it became obvious to the police that he was not actually staying in Merseyside in January of 2009, they circulated his description all over the country in September to locate him. Unfortunately, it took them nine months to issue that alert and Ashleigh paid the ultimate price.

Peter Chapman was sentenced to life in prison. The judge made it clear that he would have to serve thirty-five years before he could get a chance for a parole. Ashleigh's family, especially her mother, was deeply saddened by what happened. Her mother hoped that Facebook would take online security more seriously, and that what had happened to her daughter could be used as an example to eradicate online predators, especially pedophiles, from social media sites.

Chapter 19: Korena Roberts

Since its launch, Craigslist has made it so much easier to find items for sale and services at lower prices. Unfortunately, some people on Craigslist might also be looking for their next victim. One of these opportunists was Korena Roberts. She wanted a baby, and when she found a pregnant woman on Craigslist, she thought it was her chance to finally get what she wanted.

Korena Elaine Roberts was obsessed with everything related to babies. She already had two children from previous relationships, but in 2007, she gave birth to a stillborn. Since that time, she had been watching YouTube videos of births, sewing clothes for babies, and she even went as far as telling people that she was pregnant with twins. Korena lived with her boyfriend, Yan Shubin, in Portland, Oregon. She told him that she was pregnant in November 2008 and she was suffering from morning sickness. She was taking prenatal vitamins, scheduling ultrasound appointments, and even attending midwife classes.

Twenty-one-year-old Heather Megan Snively actually was pregnant. She was in her eighth month of pregnancy with a baby boy she planned to name John Stephen. Heather was originally from St. Albens, West Virginia, but she had recently moved to Tigard, Oregon to be with her fiancé, Christopher Popp. As any other expecting woman, Heather was very excited to have her first baby. Early in the month of June in 2009, she sent a postcard to her grandmother saying: *"Can you believe Mom and Dave are going to be grandparents?"* She did not know what awful fate was waiting for her. It all started with a few innocent clicks.

One day, Heather logged onto Craigslist to look for things she could purchase for her baby. She had used her phone number and her Yahoo email account to sign in. It was there she met Korena Roberts, the woman obsessed with babies. When Heather responded to an ad for baby items, Korena told Heather that she was also pregnant and they agreed to exchange baby clothes. After almost a week of exchanging emails, the date was set: they would meet on June 5, 2009.

When the day came, Heather went to Korena's house in Washington County. Her neighbors later reported they spotted a pregnant woman at the house with Korena. Once inside, Korena brutally attacked Heather. The autopsy would later show that Heather was bitten (she had bite marks on her elbow), and viciously beaten. It was apparent that Heather put up a fight because she left a five-inch-long scratch on the left side of her attacker's neck and injuries on her arms. Korena then used a sharp object to make an incision on Heather's womb and ripped the baby boy from her body. Heather died from blood loss and Korena stuffed her body in a crawlspace at her home.

After hiding Heather's body, Korena called her boyfriend. Earlier that day, Yan had arrived at work in the early morning around 6:00 a.m. Five hours later, he had returned home for lunch where Korena made him a sandwich. He did not notice anything out of the ordinary. At 2:30 p.m. Yan had left his work and was at the bank when he received a frantic call from Korena. She seemed as if she was in pain, and told him that she needed him. Yan hurried home. When he got there, he saw blood covering the floor. He rushed to the bathroom. There he saw Korena sitting in the bathtub with the water running, wearing only a bra. She was holding a lifeless little fragile body. Yan took the baby from her and started CPR in an attempt to save him, but he was not successful. When the paramedics arrived, they were alarmed by the amount of blood in the house and immediately took Korena and the baby to the Providence St. Vincent Medical Center. At the hospital, the doctors examined the baby and determined that he was dead. The police were called in. Korena told the police that she had been pregnant with twins and Yan thought there was a possibility the other baby might still be at the house. A team of officers went to the residence to search for another baby. At first, Korena refused to be examined, but the doctors were able to complete the exam and were stunned to realize she had not given birth any time recently. A psychological evaluation was ordered, and the psychologist later concluded she was not suffering from any mental disorders.

While the police went back to the house, Korena told Yan she "did a horrible thing." It was then Yan called the police from the hospital. He suggested they look in the crawlspace of their home, where police discovered Heather's corpse. They could see that her abdomen had been sliced open. The autopsy results revealed she had suffered blunt force trauma. The medical examiner determined that Korena had used a collapsible police baton to beat Heather to near death. Heather received between fifteen and thirty blows, most of them to the back of her head. The beating knocked her unconscious, but ultimately it was the loss of blood that killed her. It was not revealed what did Korena used to slice open Heather's abdomen, but Yan told the police that he bought a pack razor blades a few days before the murder that had gone missing. There were cuts on Heather's right breast and her abdomen. Her right arm was bitten, possibly during the struggle between the two. It was also determined that the baby boy did not take a single breath outside the womb.

Korena was arrested and charged with the murder of Heather Snively. However, since the baby did not survive the attack, Korena was only charged with one count of aggravated murder—meaning she was trying to steal the baby and killed Heather in the process. According to the laws in Oregon, a human being is "a person who has been born and was alive at the time of the criminal act." Since the state could not prove baby John had "born alive," he was not considered a person but rather as an item or a piece of property to be stolen. This is why Korena was not charged with the murder of John Stephen. During the investigation, it was discovered that Korena had previously contacted other pregnant women and had set up meetings with them, but none of the other women showed up; Heather was the unlucky victim.

In August 2009, Korena stood in court to hear the accusations and began sobbing. She was charged with one count of murder, four counts of aggravated murder, and two counts of first-degree robbery. She remained in jail without bail. At first Korena steadfastly denied killing Heather, but in 2010, she pleaded guilty to one count of aggravated murder. Korena said, "I am taking responsibility because I am guilty." She was sentenced to life in prison without the chance of parole. Her pleading guilty meant that there was no trial and that she would not face the death penalty. The guilty plea and final sentence were the result of the negotiations between the prosecution and the defense. The defense wanted to leave a chance for parole later, but the prosecution did not agree to this. They wanted to make sure Korena would never be released and would not have any chance for an appeal.

Heather Snively's mother said that all that her daughter wanted was just to exchange clothes. She also added that Heather was a trusting person and that it was a mistake to meet Korena like that. Kevin Snively, Heather's father, wished that he could get his daughter and his grandson back, but he insisted that justice should be served to the woman who took them from him. Christopher, Heather's longtime boyfriend and fi-ancé, was devastated. In a statement, he had expressed his desire to see Korena receive the death penalty. The family wished that Korena would never forget what she had done and that it would haunt her for the rest of her life. It sure would haunt them.

Chapter 20: The Long Island Serial Killer

On May 1, 2010, twenty-four-year-old Shannan Gilbert placed a call to 911 at 4:51 a.m. While the call has never been released to the public, those who have heard it claim the terrified woman tells the operator that someone is after her and is trying to kill her. The operator asks Shannan where she is, but Shannan never reveals her exact location. Because of this, the call was transferred to the New York State Police, not the local Suffolk County department. Male voices are allegedly heard on the recording trying to calm her down—a Long Island man who hired her on Craigslist as his escort for that night, Joseph Brewer, and the man who drove her to the job, Michael Pak.

Screaming, Shannan ran from Brewer's house, ending up on the doorstep of neighbor Gus Colletti. While still on the phone with the 911 operator, Shannan banged on his door. When Gus asked her what was wrong, he said she simply stared at him and repeated, "Help me" over and over. Gus

131

RJ PARKER | JJ SLATE

called 911 from his own phone and instruct-
ed Shannan to sit down while they waited
for the police to arrive. Instead, Shannan
darted out of his house, running towards another neighbor's home.

At this point, Michael Pak was spotted
chasing after her in his black SUV, trying to
coax her back into his vehicle. Shannan
banged frantically on the door of Barbara
Brennan's home, who also called police. By
the time police arrived at the scene, it was
already 5:40 a.m. and since Shannan's call
had been transferred to another department,
the only information they had to go on were
the two calls placed by Gus and Barbara. By
that time, Shannan was nowhere to be seen
and the black SUV was gone as well. Police
concluded that she must have gotten into the
vehicle at some point and left the area.
There was nothing more to be done.

When Shannan's family reported her
missing, police finally began to connect the
dots and located her twenty-three-minute
call to 911. They began searching the remote
areas near Long Island Beach in hopes of locating her. What they would find over the

next year and a half during their search would rock the beach town community to its core. Remains of ten individuals, eight of them women, one male, and one female toddler, were discovered in marshy areas spread out along three counties along Gilgo Beach, Oak Beach, and Jones Beach State Park. None of those bodies belonged to Shannan. Suddenly, investigators had a much bigger case to solve.

In November 2011, police announced they believed that one individual was responsible for all ten murders. The identified victims included five young women in their twenties that had been reported missing between 2005 and 2010: Jessica Taylor, Maureen Brainard-Barnes, Melissa Barthelemy, Megan Waterman, and Amber Lynn Costello. Like Shannan Gilbert, who was still missing at that time, all five victims had been using Craigslist to advertise their escort and prostitution services.

Amber Costello's roommate said that the night she went missing, a client had offered her $1,500 for her services, nearly six times her usual rate. He had also been persistent, pressuring her to meet him out even after she seemed wary of going. Many people involved in the case believe the killer uses Craigslist to find his victims and lure them into a deadly attack late at night. He then discards their bodies all in the same area. Police believe the other unidentified victims were also linked to prostitution, but a direct link to their identities or Craigslist has never been established. It is quite possible those victims were killed before Craigslist was founded in 1995.

The five unidentified remains include an Asian male wearing woman's clothing, who likely worked as a prostitute at the time of his death. He was killed with violent blows to the head, unlike the other murder victims who were likely strangled. Also discovered were a mother and her toddler daughter, who may have accompanied her mother on a job. Another set of remains was connected to a pair of legs that had been discovered in a plastic bag nearly a decade earlier on Fire Island. A final unidentified female victim was also linked to the other victims, after her head, right foot, and hands were located.

The rest of her body had been discovered in Manorville, New York in 2000, near the area where Jessica Taylor's torso was later found in 2003.

Shannan Gilbert's remains were eventually found in a marsh in 2011, nineteen months after the search for her began. Despite the fact that Shannan was an escort who advertised her services on Craigslist, just like the five identified victims, police don't believe she was killed by the same person. They suggest that she may have stumbled into the thick marsh and drowned while she was running that night. Shannan's family vehemently disagrees with this conclusion and insists that she is the killer's eleventh victim.

Melissa Barthclcmy's teenage sister later told the media that the killer had used her sister's cell phone to call her several times and taunt her. Melissa disappeared in July of 2009, but her sister, Amanda, received at least seven disturbing and vulgar phone calls from a man using Melissa's phone after the disappearance. In the final call, he admitted that he had killed Melissa, crushing the family's hopes of ever finding her alive. Melissa's body was one of the first to be discovered in December of 2010. Police traced the calls from the victim's cell phone and determined they were originating from the Manhattan Times Square area.

Police have released little information about what they know about the killer, dubbed by some as the Long Island Serial Killer (LISK) or the Gilgo Beach Killer (GBK), but what we do know is terrifying. The ten victims were murdered between the years 1996 and 2010. It is clear that the killer targets prostitutes in the Long Island area, likely soliciting their services from Craigslist. While it is difficult to pinpoint cause of death in most of the victims, police believe that the majority of the women were likely strangled or beaten and then dismembered. Several of the victims were disposed of in burlap sacks or plastic bags.

In April of 2011, *The New York Times* reported it is likely the serial killer is a white male between the ages of twenty-five and forty-five. FBI profilers and serial killer experts believe he may even be married or have a stable girlfriend. He is probably an educated and well-spoken individual. He is employed, financially secure, and possibly works at a job that would give him access to burlap sacks, such as landscaping, contracting, or fishing.

Some believe that the killer may be an ex-cop who is familiar with investigative techniques. The taunting calls that were made to Melissa Barthelemy's sister were all traced to crowded areas in the city where surveillance video would be useless. The killer also kept the calls under three minutes, indicating he may have known it takes between three and five minutes to trace a call. In addition, the killer took the time to dismember and dispose of his earliest victims in a scrupulous manner, perhaps indicating some knowledge that this course of action would hinder the investigation.

Other FBI profilers and serial killer experts suspect the killer may be a seasonal vacationer to the Long Island area. Since the five identified victims all went missing in the summer months, it is possible the killer has his own vacation home or visits his parents' home in the area each year. Many believe the locations of the disposal sites indicate his familiarity with the area. It is possible the killer grew up in the Long Island area and returns each summer.

Are any of these assumptions about the killer true? We won't know anything until the police solve the decades-old mystery and bring an end to his reign of terror. For years, many residents living in the Long Island community seemed to be holding their breath, waiting—would the killer strike again? Or would police be able to solve the mystery before more bodies turned up?

In July of 2014, police arrested a Manorville, New York resident named John Bittrolff for two decades-old cold case murders they say are unrelated to the LISK murders. In 1993, thirty-one-year-old Rita Tangredi's body was discovered in a housing development in East Patchogue, New York. Three months later, the body of twenty-year-old Colleen McNamee was discovered near the William Floyd Parkway in Shirley, New York. Both had been known to work as prostitutes and both bodies were strangled, beaten, and discarded in a wooded area. In addition, each woman was missing a particular article of clothing (the type of which has not been disclosed to the public). Police were also investigating Bittrolff's possible involvement with another 1993 murder in Suffolk County, that of Sandra Costilla, whose body was discovered in the small settlement of North Sea, New York. All three women were killed in a similar way and their bodies were left in similar positions, according to police.

Probably one of the most remarkable aspects of this particular arrest was not the length of time that had passed since the murders, but how this arrest came to be. Bittrolff's brother, Timothy, was arrested in 2013 and convicted of an unrelated assault. When investigators ran Timothy's DNA through their systems, as is routine for convicted offenders, the analyst realized that his DNA was extremely close to the DNA collected from Tangredi's and McNamee's unsolved murders. So close, in fact, that the killer must have had the same parents as the man they already had in custody. From there, investigators were able to track down Timothy's brother, John, whose DNA matched perfectly from the two crime scenes.

So what does all this have to do with the Long Island Serial Killer? Police are saying it's too early to link him any of the murder victims discovered in the Gilgo Beach area and they stress it is likely the two are completely unrelated. Suffolk County District Attorney Thomas Spota told the media that "the evidence recovered from Tangredi and McNamee, the manner in which their bodies were found, and the crime scenes are unique to them and distinctly different from the Gilgo crime scenes."

But there are some experts who believe there is a chance all of these victims are connected, including retired NYPD Lt. Commander Vernon Geberth. In fact, there *is* a rather large connection that the police have failed to discuss with the media—mainly that torsos from two of the LISK victims were recovered in the Manorville pine barrens, a mere three miles from where John Bittrolff has lived for over a decade.

In November of 2000, a decomposing body of a woman was discovered in garbage bags in a wooded area off Halsey Manor Road in Manorville, NY. She was approximately 5'2" and between the ages of eighteen and thirty-five years old. Her identity remains unknown. Her head and her hands were missing.

In 2003, another female body was found in the Manorville pine barrens. She too was found headless, with no hands, but police were able to determine her identity—it was twenty-year-old Jessica Taylor. The heads and other body parts of both Jessica and the body of the woman found in 2000 (now dubbed Jane Doe #6) were all located on Gilgo Beach in March and April of 2011. Both victims were included in the LISK body count that same year.

While these two victims were disposed of differently from the other eight LISK victims, their dismembered remains were found in such close proximity of a number of the other victims, investigators had to consider them as victims of the same murderer. And they have a distinct link to Manorville,

141

where Bittrolff was living at the time of the murders.

While police can tell the media that the crime scenes are unique and the evidence collected from the victims doesn't suggest a link, many are starting to believe the Manorville connection, the fact that all of the identified victims were prostitutes (or leading similar lifestyles), and the fact that a number of the bodies were mutilated or dis-membered in some way are three obvious links. In addition to Jessica Taylor and Jane Doe #6, four other victims were found in the Manorville area between the years of 2000 and 2012 (two more females and two males). In all, there are a total of seventeen bodies possibly linked here—four men, twelve women, and one toddler. Speaking exclusively to channel PIX11 news in August 2014, Vernon Geberth told reporters that he believes the torsos in Manorville and at least the four bodies found on Gilgo Beach are all connected. He suspects it would be highly unlikely that two or more serial killers in the area would be using the same location to discard their bodies. What are the chances that a serial killer discarding ten bodies on the Long Island Coast also left remains from two of his victims just three miles from another serial killer's house—a killer who also murders prostitutes and kills them in a similar manner?

If Bittrolff has been killing for over twenty years and truly is the LISK, it is reasonable to assume his methods of killing and disposal of the bodies have evolved over time. Comparing the crime scenes and the manner in which the bodies were discarded doesn't seem terribly important when you are dealing with someone who started killing in his twenties and has since grown into a middle-aged man. If you add Craigslist into the equation for his later victims, it would also make sense that his methods for finding his victims have changed as social media has evolved in the past few decades.

So who is John Bittrolff anyway? And does his profile match up with what FBI experts suspect about the LISK? John Bittrolff is a forty-eight-year-old white male who has worked as a carpenter for most of his life. He grew up in Mastic Beach, New York, attending the William Floyd school system. He is a married father of two, and neighbors claimed he knew everyone in their neighborhood and has always been incredibly friendly and helpful. One of the neighbors went so far as to tell the media he was like the town "mayor." Many of these qualities seem to fit the profile of the LISK, but it's important to note that these correlations do not indicate he is the same killer that has been terrorizing Long Island for decades.

One thing is for sure—police aren't rushing this one. They charged Bittrolff with the murders of Tangredi and McNamee in July of 2014 and they are actively working to connect him to the murder of Costilla. Maybe they are just taking their time to piece together a strong case against him. Or maybe they do have some sort of evidence that clearly proves he's not the LISK and they are keeping it from the public so as not to compromise the case. Is it possible Tangredi, McNamee, and Costilla are Bittrolff's only victims? If so, what do you think made him lie dormant for twenty years? And could there really be several serial killers that have been using the Long Island area as their own personal hunting grounds for the last several decades?

Chapter 21: Christopher Dannevig

Christopher James Dannevig was born on November 4, 1989. His life seems like a long list of violent offenses strung together, precariously leading towards a culmination that was bound to be deadly. When he was five years old, Christopher was subjected to psychological testing and ultimately diagnosed with Attention Deficit Hyperactivity Disorder (ADHD). His medical records indicate he grew up suffering from depression, self-harm, substance abuse, and several behavioral issues, including aggressive behavior towards others. His relationships always seemed to end in disaster and violence.

In 2005, sixteen-year-old Christopher was arrested in New South Wales for pulling a knife on a woman taking a walk in the bushland. He sliced her with the knife and threatened to take her life, but she managed to escape when Christopher realized other people were nearby. In 2008, he managed to lure a sixteen-year-old girl into the bushland to help him find a bag he pretended he had lost in the area. As they walked deeper into the brush, he pulled a knife and physically restrained the girl. According to reports, he pinned her to the ground by sitting on top of her body. Somehow, the girl was able to break free and report the incident to police. He was sentenced to six months in prison for this attempted kidnapping.

Days after he was released on parole for that sentence, twenty-year-old Christopher Dannevig was already looking for his next victim. He set up several profiles on dating sites in an attempt to meet girls. His profiles seemed to be crafted in an attempt to make him appear harmless to others. He wrote about his favorite ice cream flavor (chocolate), how he played guitar, was a sports fan, and claimed not to be one who cared about appearances; rather he just waned to find a girl he could trust, someone who liked him for who he was. It was through an Australian dating site called Oasis Active where he set his sights on his next victim.

Nona Belomesoff was an eighteen-year-old TAFE (Technical and Further Education) student who wrote on her Oasis Active profile that she loved art, music, photography, and animals. She was taking a course on working in the animal care industry. She also wrote a tagline for her profile in typical teenage text-speak, *"I don't add ppl without a picture, feels as if im talking to myself never knoww u might be psychoo killer or sumthingg lol."* Christopher contacted Nona through Oasis Active and the two also began communicating through Facebook, where he began to learn a lot more about her, including her love for animals. After communicating with Nona for several weeks, Christopher then set up a fake Facebook account using the alias Jason Green. He claimed to be a team leader working for the Wildlife Information Rescue and Education Service (WIRES). Soon after friending Nona under this fake account, 'Jason' offered her a job with WIRES. Over the next several weeks, the two planned to meet up at the Leumeah train station to begin a series of meetings over several days as a recruitment process. The two met five separate times during a five-day period from May 6 through May 10, 2010. During those meetings, they would walk along a path near the bushland and talk. On one of the last meetings, Nona later told her family that 'Jason' had asked her if she knew self-defense and had physically pushed her to the ground, lying on top of her. Once he released her, he said he wanted to teach her how to fight back, in case she was ever kidnapped or raped. Nona claimed he then tied her hands behind her back and blindfolded her. He then pushed her to the ground and asked, "What would you do?" After Nona began to cry and become upset, Christopher released her, apologized, and offered to call an ambulance. Nona declined.

Despite this seemingly violent and unsettling encounter, Nona agreed to meet 'Jason' again two days later, under the ruse that this time they would meet up with several of his colleagues for an overnight camping trip, which would serve as the final stage for her recruitment into WIRES. Nona told her mother that she would be compensated for her time on the overnight trip. It would be the first time she had ever slept away from home.

On May 12, Nona met up with Christopher at their usual spot in Leumeah for the fictional training camp. Despite his earlier claims that two of his colleagues from WIRES would accompany them on the camping trip, Christopher arrived alone. When Nona did not return home the next day, her concerned family reported her missing to the Liverpool police. On May 14, police spoke with Christopher, who told them that the last time he had seen Nona was on Monday, May 10. He attempted to give investigators an alibi for his whereabouts on the day Nona disappeared, but the police were unable to corroborate his account. They also uncovered that Nona's bank account had been accessed via an ATM at the Leumeah train station on the evening of May 12. Someone had requested an account balance and then withdrew the maximum amount allowed, $170.00. Surveillance footage showed that person to be Christopher Dannevig.

When confronted with this information, Christopher admitted he had taken Nona's purse and stolen the money from her ac-

151

count after learning what her PIN number was. On Friday, May 14, he was arrested. He later led investigators to a remote area in the Smith Creek Reserve, where Nona's body was located. She was fully clothed, was wearing a sleeping mask covering her eyes, and her face was partially submerged in the creek. Most of her belongings were scattered around her.

Christopher admitted to police he had created the fake Jason Green profile to be-friend Nona after learning about her love for animals. He told them that he was the only one with Nona when she died, but he wasn't quite sure what had happened. According to his version of events, the two had been sit-ting side by side on the creek bed when he suddenly "blacked out." When he became aware of his surroundings, he claimed that Nona was lying face down in the water. He told police he stood there for about 30 to 120 seconds, watching her body, but took no actions to pull her out of the water or at-tempt to resuscitate her. He then took her bankcard from her purse and left her body where it was.

Unfortunately, the medical examiner could not pinpoint the exact way Nona had died. Her body was in relatively good condition, not indicative of having put up a fight with an attacker. Her death was ruled as a drowning, and Christopher was arrested.

In a recorded conversation with an undercover officer in prison, Christopher changed his story, claiming he had gotten into an argument with Nona near the creek and he had pushed her. He stated she had fallen, hitting her head on the rocks before he held her face underwater for two minutes, drowning her.

During his trial, Christopher's attorneys claimed that he had not met Nona that day intending to kill her. However, the prosecution argued that Christopher's actions to befriend the victim using the fake profile and persona of someone working in the animal care field showed he had taken the time to cultivate a relationship in order to gain her trust. In addition, his actions two days prior to the fatal attack showed an escalating behavior of violence. The fact that the victim was found with a blindfold over her eyes gives credence to the earlier story Nona told her family—that 'Jason' had been trying to teach her self-defense tactics before her death. This goes directly against Christopher's claim that the two had been sitting and talking before he "blacked out."

Christopher's lawyers also tried to claim that he had a mild intellectual disability that could have played a role in his behavior. He was given an Adaptive Behavioral Test, which indicated that his cognitive reasoning and adaptive behavior skills were significantly compromised and, in a sense, he was mentally disabled. However, he was never diagnosed with any particular disorder or illness.

In August 2011, Christopher pleaded guilty to Nona's murder. He was sentenced to twenty-one years in prison. He will be eligible for parole in August 2032, just a few months shy of his forty-third birthday.

In response to this horrific case, a Facebook spokesman spoke out against the crime. "This case serves as a painful reminder that all internet users must use extreme caution when contacted over the internet by people they do not know. We echo the advice of the police who urge people not to meet anyone they have been contacted by online unless they know for certain who they are, as there are unscrupulous people in the world with malevolent agendas."

Chapter 22: Philip Markoff

Philip Haynes Markoff was born on February 12, 1986 and grew up in Sherill, New York. His father, Richard Markoff, was a dentist working in Syracuse, New York. He was the younger brother of Jon Markoff. After the divorce of his parents, he stayed with his mother, Susan Haynes, while his father took custody of his older brother.

As a child, Philip was a good student and well behaved. Growing up, this did not change. In his high school years, he was seen as popular and involved in various student activities; he was a member of the History Club, the bowling team, the golf team, the Youth Court, and the National Honor Society. In 2004, Philip graduated from Vernon-Verona-Sherrill High School. Others described as a smart student and a nice guy. He was also good looking. When it came to education, Philip was serious in high school and continued that reputation in college. After his graduation from high school, he went to SUNY Albany pre-med school. Three years later, in 2007, he graduated with a bachelor's degree in biology. Socially, Philip kept more to himself because he was constantly studying. For fun, he would spend a few rare nights playing poker with his friends.

Philip volunteered at the emergency room in the Albany Medical Center Hospital, where he met Megan McAllister, who was older than him by two years, in 2005. They started dating and on May 17, 2008, they became engaged. They set the date for their marriage as August 14, 2009. After graduation, Philip was accepted to Boston University Medical School. Megan was accepted to St. Kitts in the Caribbean, but she decided to postpone her studies until after the wedding.

Philip and Megan were pretty different—she wanted a first class wedding while he was in debt and lived on borrowed money. Due to their lack of money, Philip and Megan often stayed at home and did not go out much. According to Megan, Philip didn't have a lot of friends.

Despite being known as a nice guy and never having a criminal record, Philip had a dark side no one, not even Megan, knew about. It is believed he began prowling Craigslist's exotic ads for victims in early 2009, during his second year in medical school.

On April 10, 2009, Philip replied to an ad for a massage placed by Trish Leffler under the exotic services section on Craigslist. They met at the Westin Hotel in Boston, Massachusetts, where Trish had booked a room. She met him in the hallway first, and when she thought he looked safe enough, she let him into her room. As he had told her before, he looked like a college student. After letting him in, she turned around to find him pointing a gun at her. He forced her to lie down on her stomach and he tied her hands behind her back using a plastic zip-tie. He told her that he was just there for the money and that he did not intend to hurt her. He was able to steal $800 in cash, but she begged him not to take her bankcard so she wouldn't be left without any money. Before he left, he deleted some numbers on her phone, took two pairs of her thongs, tied her to the bathroom door, and put duct tape on her mouth. After he left, she was able to free herself and call for help. The police checked for any fingerprints left by the attacker, took Trish's phone as evidence, and asked her to look through the hotel's surveillance videotapes to identify the man.

Four days later, on April 18, twenty-five-year-old Julissa Brisman was found dead in the doorway of her room at the Marriott Copley Hotel in Boston. She was a masseuse who had also placed an ad for her services on Craigslist. A man using the name 'Andy' had contacted her concerning her ad, and they agreed to meet at 10:00 p.m. that night. Julissa had an arrangement with her friend Beth that she would text her when she finished the massage as a security measure, but Beth never got that text. Police were called to the hotel after guests reported hearing screams coming from a room. Julissa was found with her hands bound with a zip-tie, in her underwear, covered in blood. According to the medical examiner, Julissa was hit on her head with an object, and then shot three times: in the chest, stomach, and heart. It appeared that she resisted her attacker because she was bruised on her wrists and was able to scratch him. The skin found under her nails provided the police with the DNA of Julissa's killer. The police also went through the surveillance footage where they found a familiar man: the same one who attacked Trish. When Julissa failed to text Beth, her friend became worried. She called the hotel to ask if someone could check on her friend and was directed to the police. Beth gave the investigators the cell phone number and the email address of 'Andy,' which proved to be a huge contribution to the advancement of the investigation.

Once investigators concluded they had a serial attacker and killer on their hands, they released the pictures and a statement to the public about the crimes. The case instantly gained national media coverage as stories began circulating about a new 'Craigslist killer.'

Only two days later, the killer struck again. Cynthia Melton was a stripper and also placed exotic ads on Craigslist. On April 16, she arranged to meet a man at the Holiday Inn Express in Rhode Island. As a security measure, her husband Kevin was in the room next door, waiting for her. The man arrived at 10:51 p.m. After she looked at him and decided he seemed safe enough, Cynthia let him in. When she turned around, the man was pointing a gun at her. He appeared to be nervous. As with his previous victims, he bound her hands together with zip-ties. He assured her that he was just looking for money. During that time, Kevin became concerned when his wife did not let him know that her client had arrived, so he went to check on her using a duplicate room key. As he opened the door, the man inside became startled. Kevin was surprised to see a gun pointed at him, so he backed out, tripped, and fell down. The man used this opportunity to escape.

The couple called the police and gave them a description of the man. They were also able to identify him from the footage from the hotel security camera. Investigators knew that they were looking for the same man that the Boston Police Department had issued warnings about. They now knew that their killer was choosing all his victims through Craigslist. The Rhode Island police were able to supply more images of the attacker obtained from the security cameras of a nearby Wal-Mart to aid in the investigation.

On April 18, 2009, the detectives traced the emails from 'Andy' to Philip Markoff, who was living in an apartment building in Quincy, Massachusetts. Using Facebook, the police found Philip through a page Megan had set up for their wedding. They discovered that he was a medical student at Boston University. The police compared the picture on his student I.D. to the pictures from the security cameras and put him on a twenty-four-hour surveillance watch. At a supermarket, police picked up items touched by Philip and sent his fingerprints for analysis. The two surviving victims, Trish and Cynthia, identified Philip as the man who attacked him.

On April 20, 2009, Philip and his fiancée Megan decided to take a trip to Foxwoods Casino in Connecticut. On the way there, police pulled over the car and arrested Philip for the murder of Julissa Brisman. Both

Philip and Megan were taken in for questioning. Megan was convinced that they had the wrong man and fully cooperated with the police because she felt there was nothing to hide. On the other hand, Philip was being difficult during the interrogation.

Megan didn't believe that the man she was going to marry was actually a killer until the police searched their apartment and found more evidence. Inside a hollowed out copy of the book *Gray's Anatomy of the Human Body,* police found a gun. Philip had purchased the gun using a driver's license with the name 'Andrew Miller,' the same name he used with his victims. Investigators also found bullets that matched the ones used in the murder of Julissa. Moreover, they found plastic zip-ties, duct tape, unused disposable TracFone cell phones purchased in February of the same year, and sixteen pairs of panties under the mattress, including the two stolen from Trish. They also found on his laptop some fragments of communication with Julissa.

It was also discovered that Philip was using a Yahoo email address (sexaddict5385@yahoo.com) in the Spring of 2008 to exchange sexually explicit photos and messages with strangers until January 2009. He had also registered in a BDSM website for alternative lifestyles under the transvestitism category and he listed himself as preferring a submissive sexual role.

On April 21, Philip was charged with the murder of Julissa Brisman, among other weapons and burglary charges. He was sent to Nashua Street Jail and ordered held without bail. Philip pleaded not guilty. Two days later, he tried to commit suicide using his shoelaces. He was put on suicide watch.

On April 29, Megan visited Philip in jail and broke off their engagement. The next day, Philip tried to kill himself again. He used a sharpened metal spoon to try and cut his wrists, but he was unable to cause serious harm to himself. By June, he seemed to be feeling better and was mixing with other inmates. However, when Megan visited one more time and told him that she was going through with her plans to go to med-school in the Caribbean and she was unlikely to ever see him again, Philip attempted suicide again by taking an overdose of antianxiety pills prescribed to him by the prison's psychiatrist. He was again put on suicide watch.

On August 15, 2010, one day after what would have been his first anniversary with Megan, Philip finally succeeded in killing himself. In his cell, he spread out pictures of his ex-fiancée on the table. With his blood, he wrote the words "Megan" and "Pocket" (the nickname he used to call her when they were together) above the doorway. Then, Philip slashed major arteries on his legs and ankles, and his carotid artery in his neck. He also placed a plastic bag over his head to suffocate himself after swallowing toilet paper so he could not be resuscitated. Then, he covered himself with blankets and lay down on his bed to die.

On September 16, 2010, the prosecutors were forced to legally drop the charges, as the defendant was deceased. The case was considered closed, and on March 31, 2011, they released 120 pieces of evidence against him to the public. The evidence included the brown leather shoes he was wearing when he was arrested, which were splattered with the blood of Julissa Brisman.

Chapter 23: David Kelsey Sparre

Like many criminals profiled in this book, David Kelsey Sparre led a troubled childhood. His father was sent to prison when he was just a young child and his mother married seven different times, jumping from relationship to relationship, always putting her men before her son. He suffered physical and emotional abuse at a young age and turned to drugs and alcohol before he had even reached his teenage years. He joined the ROTC in high school, but dropped out before he graduated.

An active user of online dating sites, David had profiles on woome.com, lavalife.com, and datehookup.com. In his dating profiles, he claimed to enjoy working out, loved children, and was seeking "a good hookup." David also frequented the Craigslist personal ads, looking for women to date.

Meanwhile, twenty-one-year-old Tiara Pool lived in Jacksonville, Florida with her husband, Michael, and two sons, Kenyon

RJ PARKER | JJ SLATE

and Kaeden. Michael worked as a technician for gas turbine systems at the Mayport Naval Station and was often deployed for duty out on the ships for extended periods of time. In 2010, Tiara and her husband were trying to keep a struggling marriage alive. Her two children, ages one and three, were living with their grandparents while she tried to finish up school. She was hoping to graduate in September of 2010 and was planning to join the Navy Reserves.

While her husband was out at sea, she posted an ad on Craigslist looking for a companion. David, then a nineteen-year-old living in Georgia at the time, responded to the ad and the two began communicating via text messages. They chatted for nearly a week before they finally decided to meet in Tiara's town in Jacksonville, Florida. David told her that he was headed to St. Vincent's Medical Center to drop his grandmother off for heart surgery (which was actually a true story) and that's where the two decided to meet.

On July 8, 2010, David drove his grandmother to the hospital. Surveillance video shows David walking around the hospital before Tiara arrived. After the two met, they eventually left the hospital together and headed back to Tiara's home in her car.

At some point, the two became intimate. Afterwards, David stabbed her eighty-nine times in her neck, back, and head, leaving her body on her bedroom floor naked. The medical examiner later found the tip of the knife embedded into her skull. The blade had been bent from the violent attack. Tiara actually survived most of the attack and only died once the deep cuts into her back were made.

David stayed in the home for some time after the murder, cleaning up the scene and looking for things to steal. He then drove back to the hospital in Tiara's vehicle and sent two text messages to her phone saying, "don't bother coming I can't leave," and "guess you're mad at me."

After not hearing from her friend for four days, Michelle Edwards arrived at Tiara's home to check on her welfare. She entered the house and looked around. According to Michelle's later testimony, when she opened

171

the door to the bedroom, she saw Tiara's hand on the floor. She spun around immediately and ran out of the house.

Police later located Tiara's car near the hospital and found surveillance video of her meeting up with David. Computer and phone records led them straight to him. He was arrested on July 24, just a few weeks after the murder took place, when police located him at a family member's home in Charleston, South Carolina. According to police, David confessed to the murder after he was arrested, but he declined to say why he had brutally killed Tiara.

During the trial, David's defense team tried to convince the jury that after the two had consensual sex, Tiara had revealed to him that she was married with two children. His lawyers claimed that he had blacked out with rage upon hearing this news and when he came to, Tiara's body lay in a crumpled mess of blood and mangled flesh on the bedroom floor. The prosecution disputed that evidence wholeheartedly, saying that David had stabbed Tiara dozens of times with the biggest knife he could find in her kitchen, and then remained in the apartment for some time, cleaning up the crime scene. He later bragged to others that he was an expert on forensic investigations and knew how to clean up a crime scene from watching TV shows. He also stole several things from Tiara's home before leaving, including her husband's PlayStation 3 console, which he sold to a pawnshop when he returned to Georgia.

The jury spent just twenty-five minutes in deliberation before rejecting the defense's argument of second-degree murder. Instead, they convicted him of first-degree murder.

During the penalty phase, David went against the advice of his attorneys and waived his right for witnesses to testify in his defense during the sentencing phase. Because of this, he lost out on the possibility of showing mitigating factors that may have contributed to his violent acts, such as abuse he allegedly suffered at a young age, his early exposure to drugs and alcohol, and any medical conditions. It only took the jury an hour to agree upon giving twenty-year-old David Sparre the death penalty. According to reports from those in the courtroom, David smiled widely when he heard their recommendation.

Shortly after the jury recommended a death sentence, a letter David wrote to his ex-girlfriend from prison leaked to the media. In it, he claimed he had planned the murder at least a week before he began looking for a victim. He knew he was going to be in Jacksonville that week and had purposely looked online for a victim in that area. He claimed he killed Tiara "for the rush" and not only did he enjoy it, but he hoped to one day do it again. He also claimed to be a member of the Crips, a rival gang of the Bloods, and his very first murder was an initiation shooting of a member in the rival gang. Any truth behind these claims has yet to be proven. The prosecution successfully admitted the letter into evidence before Circuit Judge Elizabeth Senterfitt made her ruling decision to determine his fate. On March 30, 2012, she sentenced him to death.

In December of 2013, David's lawyers filed an appeal with the Florida Supreme Court, asking his death sentence be thrown out on the grounds that the state should have allowed the court to hear testimony about mitigating factors in his case, even though the defendant waived that right. The appeal has potential to change the way death penalty cases are handled in Florida—should a court hear testimony on mitigating factors even after the defendant waives his or her right? At the time of this writing, no decision had been made by the Florida Supreme Court.

Chapter 24: Chris Dean

Some people use the internet to run scams and steal money from others online. But when the victims strike back, things can turn deadly. In 1998, such a case made national headlines in the United States.

Chris Dean grew up in Michigan. In his late twenties, he earned his commercial driver's license and started working in hauling steel. A few years later, he moved to Pierceton, Indiana with his second wife, Diane. For a while, he had a job at Little Bighorn, a golf club in Pierceton. In 1995, he began working with the Sprint North Supply Company, driving a flatbed truck carrying spools of telephone cables for delivery.

In Pierceton, he was known at the Little Bighorn Golf Club as competitive, but good humored. His neighbors remembered him as obsessively neat, always washing his cars, taking care of his lawn, and keeping the house clean. Dean also was interested in radios and often frequented the CB shops in the area. He was a licensed ham (amateur radio) operator, and was always considerate on air. Dean also liked to hunt. At an academy at Pierceton, he took *taekwondo* lessons.

Online, Chris Dean encountered seventeen-year-old Chris Marquis, a high school dropout. Marquis had used different identities online, such as 'Psycho' or 'Taz' or 'PhantomOp,' but this time he pretended to be a twenty-seven-year-old married father and owner of an online company, the CB Shack. In reality, Marquis was living with his mother and had a condition that made his eyesight so weak he couldn't see at night. Using an online identity made Marquis feel invincible. He used these identities that he created to make deals with people online looking to trade different types of radios. However, when the people sent him the items, Marquis would either not send anything back or he would send some old or broken items. Marquis was unlucky enough to cross paths with Chris Dean.

Dean and Marquis made a deal—Dean would send a Ranger RCI 2990, which was worth at least $800, and in return Marquis would send back a Cobra 2000 CB radio, which was only worth about $400. Although the deal was shady from the beginning, since Dean would receive something of half of the value of what he was sending (there were some claims that Dean actually stole the equipment from a CB shop owner in Pierceton), Marquis went along with the deal, knowing he would benefit from it. Dean was honest with the plan and sent Marquis the 2990. However, Marquis sent him back a Realistic mobile radio that was broken and did not even work. When Dean received this radio, he began calling Marquis to threaten him and he also sent hostile emails. He also warned him that he would come to Vermont to find Marquis and get his money back. Even with all the threats, Marquis was sure that his mother would protect him, as she had always done before. After all, Marquis' mother would do anything for him.

Meanwhile, Dean began planning his revenge. He had talked with a friend, who would later help with the police investigation by cooperating, about whether he would pay Marquis a threatening visit or send him a surprise package. The friend did not know exactly what Dean would send; in actuality, everyone was surprised to find out.

On March 19, 1998, a UPS driver delivered a package to Marquis' house in Fair Haven, Vermont. Marquis was talking with his girlfriend, Cyndi McDonald, using the radio Dean had sent him, so his mother intercepted the package. She brought the package up to Marquis' room. Neither of them recognized the return address or the name on the box: Samantha Brown, 1863 South High Street, Bucyrus, Ohio. As Marquis opened the package with his jackknife, he found a smaller box inside which was made of Styrofoam. Suddenly, there was an explosion and both Marquis and his mother were knocked to the floor. Marquis died on his way to the hospital and his mother was seriously injured. The bomb severely injured her legs and she spent over a year in a wheelchair.

The investigation about the bombing began immediately. FBI agents became involved. While searching Marquis' room, the agents found a piece of paper with Dean's phone number and address. In Marquis' wallet, they found a UPS receipt with the date March 5, 1998, the details of the shipment of the radio to Indiana (the same address written on the paper found earlier), and the tracking number, which let them know that the package was sent through UPS from Rutland on March 5 and it was delivered to Pierceton on March 11 at 1:56 p.m. The name and the address written on the package containing the bomb were a dead end—the person and the street did not exist. However, the FBI discovered that the bomb was dropped off around noon on March 18 in a counter facility in Mansfield, Ohio and it was shipped the next day.

According to Dean's employer, Dean's truck route included Michigan, Indiana, and Ohio. Moreover, around noon on March 18, Dean had been delivering goods to a warehouse in Mansfield, Ohio, which would have enabled him to pass through Bucyrus, Ohio and drop off the package. Dean's unidentified friend told Special Agent John Hersh that Dean was very interested in CB radios

181

and that he had been having some trouble with a guy in Vermont with whom he exchanged radios. It was also found that Dean had looked up instructions online to help him construct a pipe bomb.

On March 20, 1998, Chris Dean was arrested for sending the bomb that killed Chris Marquis. The entire investigation, including the arrest, took no more than thirty hours. Friends and neighbors could not believe that Dean was capable of doing such a thing, especially since he did not have a previous criminal record. He was charged with interstate transportation of an explosive device with the intention to kill and injure Chris Marquis, and endangering the lives of people aboard the aircraft that transported the package.

On March 25, it was ruled that there was enough evidence to extradite Dean to Vermont where he would be tried. On April 2, he was placed in a maximum-security facility. On June 22, Dean pleaded not guilty. However, the evidence against him was stacking up. Investigators found a Styrofoam container found at his house that matched the material used in the bomb. Moreover, hex nuts and fishing lines were also found, which were similar to the ones used in the bomb. In his backyard, there was a blast hole, which led the investigators to believe that he had built a prototype bomb and detonated it. Chris Dean was held without bail as he waited for his trial. In February 2000, Dean changed his plea to guilty in exchange for a sentence of life in prison without the chance of parole. After his guilty plea, the prosecution agreed not to pursue the death penalty. He is currently serving his sentence in a federal prison in western Virginia. While the evidence against Dean is vast, some question his innocence. Could Chris Dean have really learned how to construct a pipe bomb within a period of seven days? And, as a smart man, why did Dean leave a trail leading to him? Did police investigate and arrest their suspect too quickly? Couldn't another enemy (and there were plenty) have killed Chris Marquis?

In 2006, Chris Dean, acting as his own lawyer, filed an appeal attempting to vacate his sentence, which was denied. In response,

Chris Marquis' mother, Sheila Rockwell, sent him a card in prison. It simply read, "Congratulations, you didn't make it."

Chapter 25: Lacey Spears

Social media monsters don't just use the internet to locate and lure their victims; they also have been known to use it to exploit their victims for their own personal gain or entertainment. In the case of Lacey Spears, it is alleged she did just that—and her victim was her young son.

Lacey Spears was born on October 16, 1987, the youngest of three children to Terry and Tina Spears. She was twenty-one years old when she began a romantic relationship with Chris Hill. The two lived in the same apartment building in Decatur, Alabama in 2008. When Lacey became pregnant, the two talked about baby names and even marriage. Then one day Lacey told him that the child she was carrying was not his. She began telling friends and family that the child's father was a man named Blake—a police officer who had tragically died in a car accident. But none of Lacey's friends or family had ever met Blake, nor had they ever heard any mention of him until then.

Many of them now believe that Blake is a figment of Lacey's imagination and she made up the entire story to gain sympathy. She later created a blog devoted entirely to Blake and wrote about the impact his death had on her life. Lacey pushed Chris away and even threatened to call the police on him if he came near her. Reluctantly, Chris backed off.

On December 3, 2008, Lacey gave birth to a healthy baby boy, whom she named Garnett-Paul Thompson Spears. She continued to live in the same apartment complex as Chris, who often peered out the window when she came and went to get a glimpse of his own son that he was not allowed to see.

When Garnett was just five days old, Lacey rushed him back to the hospital. He was suffering from a severe ear infection, high fever, and he was bleeding from his nose. This would be the first of many, many hospital visits for baby Garnett. Over the years, it seemed to outsiders that Garnett was the unluckiest infant in the world, plagued with sickness after sickness. When he was just one month old, he faced surgery to help his acid reflux. At ten weeks, Lacey claimed Garnett simply stopped breathing and doctors found his sodium levels had spiked unexpectedly.

At ten months, doctors inserted a feeding tube in Garnett's abdomen because Lacey claimed he couldn't keep any food in his stomach without throwing it back up. In reality, Lacey had begged doctors at one hospital to insert the feeding tube, but they had refused to do so after nurses came forward voicing their concerns. Apparently Garnett was able to eat and digest his food just fine when Lacey was not around. Infuriated, Lacey took her baby to another hospital, where the feeding tube was inserted.

Time and time again, Garnett seemed to recover from his ailments during his hospital stays when nurses tended to him, but once Lacey took him home, something would happen and she would return to the hospital again with different symptoms. Just weeks before Garnett's first birthday, Lacey posted to Twitter, "My Sweet Angel Is In The Hospital For The 23rd Time :(Please Pray He Gets To Come Home Soon..."

In fact, Lacey was using social media a lot around this time and in the years to come. As Garnett grew older and his long list of illnesses continued, she took to the internet to build quite a large following of supporters who followed his story closely. Calling him 'Garnett-the-Great,' Lacy started a blog, 'Garnett's Journey,' where she posted publically about her son's seemingly endless list of medical issues. She kept her loyal readers of the blog updated through Twitter, MySpace, and even Facebook. In few short years of Garnett's life, Lacey built up a huge following of supporters and fans, who eagerly waited for the next post to update them about the baby's condition.

When Garnett was two years old, Lacey moved out of her apartment building in Decatur and took her son to live with her mother in Clearwater, Florida. There, she worked as a babysitter and joined a support group for parents where she would often share her account of raising a chronically ill baby. She also spoke of Blake, Garnett's fictitious father who had died in a devastating car accident, leaving her to raise her son alone.

It wasn't long after Lacey moved to Clearwater that she became a regular at the emergency room. Garnett was admitted several times for various reasons—a staph infection, high fevers, and blood coming out of his nose or ears. In 2011, two separate people contacted the Department of Children and Families in Florida to complain about Lacey's parenting ethics and that she was medically neglecting her child. In one of the complaints (from a member of the parenting group Lacey was a member of), it was alleged that Lacey would slap Garnett to make him cry before she would pick him up to soothe him. Other allegations claimed she would take the toddler swimming while his ears and eyes were bleeding, or take him on errands when he was running a fever.

Investigators questioned Lacey after these complaints were filed and took note of his disturbing medical history, but ultimately did not take any action. Garnett didn't show any physical signs of abuse and there was not much more the investigators could do. Lacey always took to her public forum whenever someone questioned her parenting skills, preaching that Garnett came first in her life and she would never do anything to harm him.

In 2012, Lacey and Garnett moved to Chestnut Ridge, New York, where she told others they were practicing holistic healing and living with a secluded group known as the Fellowship Community. The group believes in living off the land and has an exclusive community that interviewed Lacey and others who knew her extensively before accepting her into the community. With each hospital visit, Lacey would keep up with her blog entries and Facebook posts. She also began posting disturbing photos of little Garnett hooked up to machines, struggling to get well. Lacey kept him on a feeding tube, despite the fact that members of the community would witness him eating solid food with ease outside of Lacey's care in his preschool class. Lacey would tell anyone who asked that Garnett suffered from a "failure to thrive," a diagnosis given to children who couldn't gain weight properly. However, in all the years in and out of hospitals, little Garnett had never actually been diagnosed with anything concrete.

On January 12, 2014, five-year-old Garnett became ill with what seemed like the flu. Over the next eleven days, while Garnett remained confined to a hospital bed, Lacey posted online that Garnett had begun having seizures, and eventually was put on a breathing tube. She asked for prayers for her dying son, prompting a flood of messages from friends and strangers alike who followed little Garnett's life online.

On January 19, Garnett was airlifted from Nyack Hospital to the Maria Farari Children's Hospital, where he was put on life support. Lacey took a photo of Garnett attached to the breathing machine and posted it on Facebook, prompting more words of concern and prayers from her online community. An online fundraiser was started to help her raise money for medical expenses.

Doctors looking at the records sent over from Nyack Hospital told Lacey that her son's body had alarmingly high levels of sodium in it and it was "metabolically impossible" for that to occur naturally. Lacey did not have an explanation for them. On January 21, Garnett fell into a coma and never regained consciousness again. His brain had become so swollen from the levels of sodium that there was nothing more doctors could do.

Over the next two days, Lacey slept on a cot in Garnett's hospital room, where she continued to update her doting supporters on Garnett-the-Great's condition. On Thursday, January 23, Lacey wrote on Facebook, "Garnett the great journeyed onward today at 10:20 a.m." The day before his death, Lacey had contacted a neighbor in the Fellowship and asked her to go to her house and dispose of materials she had been using to feed her son through his feeding tube. The friend initially did as she was told, but contacted police soon after, when she learned of a police investigation surrounding Garnett's death.

Doctors were still alarmed at Garnett's sodium levels and had contacted the police even before the five-year-old slipped into a coma. Police were able to recover the bag Lacey had asked her neighbor to dispose of and discovered the solution she had been feeding him with contained toxic levels of salt. Lacey's cell phone was seized and investigators discovered that she had specifically researched the dangers of high levels of salt in a child.

Police also pored over videotape footage taken from Garnett's hospital room during his stay at Nyack Hospital from January 17 to 19. On the first day, Garnett appeared to be fine and the doctors informed Lacey that he would be able to go home soon if his condition continued to improve. Soon after that, footage showed Lacey removed Garnett from his bed, taking him into the bathroom while holding the connector to his feeding tube and a cup of liquid. Once he was back in bed, Garnett began to flail about in pain and throw up. Lacey continued to take Garnett to the bathroom several more times, and each time she returned him to the bed, he would scream in pain and writhe around in his bed. The video shows Lacey sitting by his bedside, watching him coldly as he screamed. It is only when a nurse entered the room that she began to comfort him. The EEG machine used to monitor Garnett's

193

brain activity showed that each time Lacey took her son into the bathroom, his sodium levels spiked dramatically.

Investigators believe that Lacey suffers from Munchausen by proxy, a psychiatric disorder in which parents will cause harm to or sicken their children for attention or sympathy from others. It may be one of the first homicide cases involving the disorder in the era of social media. They believe that Lacey had become so addicted to receiving attention from others, especially fueled by her online community, and her need to continue that attention caused her to deliver a lethal dose of sodium to her son.

Experts say that most Munchausen cases rarely end in death because once the child dies, the attention and sympathy from others will eventually end. When deaths do occur, it is usually a case of miscalculation or an accident. Many believe that this won't be the first case of Munchausen by proxy involving the internet—the public arena of social media sites enables those seeking attention to gain quite a large sympathetic audience. If it is attention these individuals seek, they can find vast amounts of doting sympathizers through online avenues.

A grand jury indicted twenty-six-year-old Lacey Spears in June of 2014 and she surrendered peacefully to police. She was charged with second-degree depraved murder and first-degree manslaughter in Garnett's death. Depraved murder is a charge that focuses more on extreme recklessness rather than intentional killing. She faces twenty-five years to life in prison if convicted. Prosecutors may have a difficult time proving probable cause, however. In early September 2014, Lacey's defense attorney, David Sachs, indicated he hoped to keep much of the key evidence police uncovered in their investigation out of the trial, including the feeding tube and bag containing lethal salt levels, Garnett's extensive medical history, as well as the tens of thousands of Facebook and blog posts detailing Garnett's short life. He is also trying to prohibit prosecutors from mentioning Munchausen by proxy during the trial. The judge presiding on the case is expected to make a ruling on these motions sometime in October 2014. It is unclear when her trial will begin.

Chapter 26: Kyle Dube

Kyle Dube (pronounced Due-bee) grew up in Orono Maine, graduating from Orono High School in 2011. He worked at the Getchell Agency, a small care provider for individuals with disabilities. He lived at home with his parents and he had a four-year-old daughter that friends said he doted on. Most who knew him claimed he was a nice, down to earth guy, but Kyle had run into problems with the law as a teenager. In 2012, he led police on a 130-mile-per-hour chase while on a motorcycle. When he slowed down, his motorcycle hit a police cruiser. He had also been arrested for theft and burglary of a motor vehicle and carrying a loaded firearm.

Even though he had a girlfriend himself, twenty-year-old Kyle was obsessed with a younger girl from a local town named Nichole Cable. A gorgeous fifteen-year-old with strawberry blond hair, Nichole lived in Glenburn, Maine, just eleven miles away from Orono. Nichole loved music and dancing and was extremely close to her family members, who affectionately called her "CoCo." Unfortunately for Kyle, Nichole had a boyfriend and even though the two had spent some time together in the spring of 2013, she wasn't interested in him romantically.

In an attempt to get closer to Nichole, Kyle created a fake Facebook account in the name of a male teen he knew casually from a nearby high school, Bryan Butterfield. Using Bryan's photos and the fake profile, Kyle friended Nichole online and the two began to talk.

On May 11, 2013, Nichole told her boyfriend via text message that Kyle had groped her and tried to kiss her. She claimed she had physically pushed him off of her, but not before he left a bite mark on her skin. Despite this claim, Nichole continued to text Kyle the next day. She was also still talking to him via the fake profile where he was posing online as Bryan Butterfield. 'Bryan' tried to get Nichole to go out with him several times, and she finally agreed when he offered to give her a free bag of marijuana.

She texted Kyle to tell him she was going to meet a guy named Bryan to get a "free 20 bag," and asked him if she should be scared to meet him. Kyle encouraged her to go. He told her to call him if she needed him for anything.

That day, May 12, Mother's Day, Nichole told her mother she was meeting a friend at the end of their street. She didn't know that Bryan Butterfield was actually Kyle Dube, wearing a ski mask and holding a roll of duct tape. He had a sinister scheme in mind. He was planning to tape her up with duct tape, kidnap her, and then happen to stumble across her later without the mask, as himself, and rescue her. Kyle thought that this plan would surely win her over—and what could go wrong? He would become her hero and the two could finally be together.

Police later found evidence of a violent struggle in the woods. It appeared as if Nichole made a run for it, but Kyle chased her down and subdued her. Nichole fought her attacker so hard, her sneakers came off her feet. Kyle taped Nichole up with duct tape and put her in the bed of his father's pickup truck. According to Kyle's version of events, when he went to take her out of the truck later, he realized she was dead. He panicked and hid her body in the woods under some brush.

When she didn't return by the next morning, Nichole's mother reported her missing to police. She feared her daughter had been lured out of the home by a stranger she had met online. A huge search party was organized and hundreds of people spent days searching the nearby area for Nichole. Her parents held a press conference in which they pleaded for her captor to return their daughter. Meanwhile, Kyle Dube posted about Nichole's disappearance on his personal Facebook account. "Please help these [sic] family get back together. Nicole [sic] wherever you are, I hope you're safe," he wrote. The next day, he posted a photo of Nichole with the words, "Help find Nichole Cable."

Police investigating Nichole's Facebook account saw her communications with 'Bryan Butterfield.' They interviewed the real Bryan Butterfield from Bangor High School, who claimed someone else had created the fake profile and used his photos. He told police that he suspected it was Kyle Dube, who wanted to hook up with Nichole but she wasn't interested in him. Police then traced the IP address from the fake profile to Kyle Dube's parents' home in Orono.

When police spoke with Kyle, they noticed he had fresh scratches on his face. He told them he had received the scratches at his place of work, where he cared for people with disabilities. Kyle denied having any contact with Nichole on the day she went missing, but his girlfriend, Sarah Mersinger, and his brother, Dustin Dube, told police that Kyle had told them he accidentally killed the girl in a botched kidnapping attempt. Dustin was the one to tell police where to look for Nichole's body. She was discovered under a pile of sticks in a wooded area a few miles from her home a week later, on May 20. A warden searching the woods with his dog made the discovery. The medical examiner determined that Nichole died from "asphyxia due to compression of the neck."

Kyle was charged with one count of murder and one count of kidnapping in the disappearance and death of Nichole Cable in June of 2013. He is currently being held without bail, awaiting his trial.

In response to the role social media played in the shocking murder of Nichole, many of her friends deactivated their Facebook accounts out of paranoia. Many of them had also been contacted by the fake 'Bryan Butterfield' account and went through their friend lists to make sure that they knew all their contacts personally. Nichole's mother, Kristin Wiley, has made it her goal to teach students how to be safe online. Since her daughter's death, she has conducted seminars for parents and teens, hoping that she can save other lives by teaching online safety measures. Kristin and her husband, Jason Wiley, also appeared on the Dr. Phil show a few months after Nichole's death. The episode was geared towards teaching teens about the dangers of meeting strangers online. "My hope is to give parents awareness and give them some safety tips, and to let them know that this can happen to anybody," she later told the media. "It can be your child and you need to take the precautions knowing every day that something could happen."

Chapter 27: Mark Andrew Twitchell

Fulfilling twisted fantasies has become much easier with the worldwide outburst of internet use. Moreover, the spread of movies and TV shows that glorify killing might seem harmless to some, but could spark an obsession in others. But most people who watch those types of shows don't actually fantasize about killing other people, right?

Mark Andrew Twitchell was born on July 4, 1979 in Edmonton, Alberta. He was an aspiring Canadian filmmaker. Mark was working on many projects, including a fan-fiction *Star Wars* film entitled *Secrets of the Rebellion* and another mystery thriller movie called *House of Cards*. In October 2005, Mark founded a film promotions company called Xpress Entertainment. The company later focused on film production. Mark was a married father, but he also had a girlfriend.

In September of 2008, Mark created a short horror movie. He had rented a garage at the south of Edmonton, where he planned to shoot the film.

Meanwhile, thirty-eight-year-old John Altinger was working for a manufacturer of oil field equipment. John was trying online dating when he met a woman on the website plentyoffish.com. On October 10, 2008, John told his friends that he was meeting this woman at a rented garage. John was expecting a date, but instead he was met by Mark who used a pipe to hit him in the head. After that, Mark stabbed John to death with a hunting knife. Later, he dismembered the body and got rid of the remaining parts in the city sewers.

John's friends became worried. They had received strange messages from him telling them that he was going on a trip to Costa Rica with that woman he met on the date. They broke into groups and searched his apartment, where they discovered his passport and realized he didn't actually pack anything for a trip. They reported him missing and the Edmonton Police Department quickly began a homicide investigation.

On October 31, 2008, Mark was arrested for the murder of John Altinger. He was charged with first-degree murder. According to Mark, he pretended to be a woman online as a prank to promote his upcoming movie. He planned on luring men into the garage. However, when John found out that it was a prank, he became angry and attacked Mark, who claimed he murdered John in self-defense. After John's death, Mark dismembered him in order to conceal his crime. However, police uncovered evidence which points in another direction.

Mark was obsessed with *Star Wars*, weapons, and he was a fan of the television series *Dexter*. The main character in the show, Dexter Morgan, worked for the fictional Miami Police Department as a blood spatter analyst by day and killed proven killers to prevent them from claiming other victims by night. It is believed that Mark was trying to bring that character to life and impersonate Dexter.

On Mark's laptop, the police found a document titled "SKConfessions," which had been deleted, but they were able to recover it. "SK" stood for serial killer. This document was presented as key evidence during Mark's trial. The opening passage in the document is: "This story is based on true events. The names and events were altered slightly to protect the guilty. This is the story of my progression into becoming a serial killer." The author described how he planned to commit a murder, how his first attempt in killing failed, and then how his second attempt succeeded. The author lured a man to a rented garage by pretending to be a woman online, then killed him, dismembered the victim, and then disposed of the remains. During the trial, Mark admitted to the murder but retained the self-defense claim. He also stated that the document was based on fiction to dramatize the work and make it more appealing.

Indeed, Mark had actually tried to kill another man before John. That man, Gilles Tetreault, managed to escape. This was all described in the document, which was made a lot more credible as prosecutors were able to show that it was based on true events. Gilles testified at the trial that he had expected to meet a woman he previously met online on the dating website plentyoffish.com (the same one used to lure

John). However, Gilles was attacked by a masked man with a stun stick.

Other disturbing entries were made in the "SKConfessions" file, including more details about the attack and murder. Mark wrote, "I grabbed his jaw with my gloved hand and moved it while making a funny voice to make it look like it was talking, and chuckled to myself at the total silliness of it all." He also made mention of religious people, writing, "I have no place for them and I find the whole concept of religion detestable. It's all a big, corrupt power grab designed to take advantage of simple-minded common folk."

Mark also discussed his opinion about killing others. "Most people fantasize and it only ever stays a fantasy. They don't have the disposition or the stomach to go all the way with their dark urges. But I do," he wrote. "I do not have any reservations about disposing of the negative people in this world who deserve a one-way ticket to the afterlife, if such a thing exits." The author found it "fascinating" to cut his victim open and watch the organs as they collapsed. He also diagnosed himself as a psychopath, but this was not presented in the trial because even if Mark wrote the diagnosis as the truth, he was not in a place to make such claims.

Mark's trial lasted three weeks and on April 12, 2011, he was sentenced to life imprisonment without the chance of a parole for at least twenty-five years. The prosecutor has not yet decided if the attempted murder charge against Gilles Tetreault will be pursued, but even with another conviction, there would be no addition to the life sentence already received.

While in prison, Mark purchased a TV for his cell and began watching the episodes of Dexter he had missed since his arrest. This created an outrage because people felt like he was being allowed to relive and fuel his fantasies. Mark was also trying to retrieve his work on his *Star Wars* fan film so he could edit it and make it public. While others are trying to help him do this, the police are doing their best to prevent it.

Chapter 28: Miranda Barbour

Although the internet has brought so many advantages to the world as a whole, at the same time it has enabled many troubled people to fulfill their sick fantasies. Sometimes, nothing can be enough to stop people from taking lives.

Miranda Kamille (Dean) Barbour was born in December of 1994. She was born in Alaska and raised in North Pole with her father, Sonny, her mother, Elizabeth, and her older sister, Ashley. Her childhood was troubled. At age four, Miranda was molested by the husband of her mother's sister who was later sentenced to fourteen years in prison for sexually abusing a minor.

At a young age, Miranda started using heroin and quickly became addicted to the drug. Her first experience as a runaway was at age twelve. After coming back home, Miranda told her mother that she had worked as a prostitute and that she had met a man called Forrest who was twenty-five years old and practiced Satanism. Miranda explained to her mother that this man now owned her and that he had made some carvings on her thigh and on the back of her neck as if he had branded her.

According to Miranda, her first experience with murder was when she was thirteen. By that time, she had already joined the satanic cult. One day, she went with the leader of that cult to an alley in order to meet with a man who owed the leader some money. There, the leader shot the man and then asked Miranda to shoot him again. When she couldn't do it, the leader put his hand on hers and together they pulled the trigger. Miranda's father says that this incident might have really happened because it was during the time when Miranda had run away from home.

By the age of fourteen, Miranda had run away from home many times and she had even spent some time in various treatment facilities for her heroin addiction. However, her father recalls later that Miranda was good at manipulation—she was intelligent and able to convince the doctors to let her out of the treatment.

Eventually Miranda's parents divorced. Sonny left town and moved to Florida while Elizabeth stayed in Alaska with Ashley and Miranda. During this time, Miranda claimed that she became pregnant while she was a member of a satanic cult. She told her mother the members of the cult had performed an in-house abortion because they did not want her to have the baby. However, when her mother took to a doctor, they could not find any signs of an abortion.

In 2011, Miranda did become pregnant. She later claimed in an interview that the father was Forrest, the second leader in the cult, but he had been killed soon after they conceived. Miranda's mother later confirmed that the man named Forrest was not dead and she was trying to determine if he was the baby's father. In March of 2012, Miranda was ordered by a court in Alaska to live under the custody of her mother's brother, Arlin, in North Carolina. She moved to her uncle's house and tried to change her life. She gave birth to a girl, started taking college courses, and got a job working at a grocery store.

Miranda now claims to have murdered at least twenty-two people in different states over the span of six years. However, although her father said that the first murder in Alaska when she was just thirteen could have really happened, he believes that other claimed murders in California and Texas are lies his daughter has made up. When she was in California and Texas, she was always with her father. Still, Miranda insists that she has killed this many people throughout her life and that she can lead the authorities to the places where the bodies were dumped. Miranda also claims that she only killed bad people, a story that echoes the plot of the TV show *Dexter*.

While some of the local authorities and FBI are investigating these claims, there is no evidence that Miranda has actually committed these murders and there are not any unsolved murders in those states. One thing is for sure: Miranda did commit at least one murder, one that could have brought death penalty charges.

After moving to Coats, North Carolina, Miranda began working at a local grocery store. There, she met Aimee Vaneyll, who was also pregnant, and her twenty-two-year-old boyfriend, Elytte "Elf" Barbour. The three of them quickly became friends. Elytte was into Satanism, just like Miranda. In March 2013, Aimee and Elytte broke up. A few months later, in June 2013, Miranda and Elytte started a relationship.

On October 22, 2013, Miranda and Elytte got married. Just three days later, they both quit their jobs and moved to central Pennsylvania with some friends. In order to pay the bills, Miranda was working as a 'companion,' meeting her clients on Craigslist. For each encounter, she would earn between $50 and $850. According to Miranda, she only had conversations with her clients—she wasn't a prostitute.

On November 1, Miranda used Craigslist to post an ad in which she offered some companionship for any man who "hated" his wife. Forty-two-year-old Troy LaFerrara answered the ad. They agreed that they would meet in the parking lot of a local mall. The date was November 11, Elytte's twenty-second birthday. Miranda was in the car waiting and Elytte hid in the backseat under a blanket. The couple agreed on a signal— when Miranda asked, "Did you see the stars tonight?" Elytte would get up and strangle Troy.

When Troy got into the car, she claimed she told him that she was sixteen years old (she was actually nineteen). When Troy said that he did not care, she knew that he was the one to kill. Miranda drove the vehicle to a secluded area, where she put it in park. She gave the signal to Elytte two times, but it wasn't until she hit him on the leg that he jumped up and began to strangle Troy using a cord. While Troy struggled to breathe, Miranda used a knife to stab him twenty times. Then the couple took his wallet, dumped the corpse in an alley, and headed to a Wal-Mart where they purchased items to clean up their car. To celebrate Elytte's birthday, they went to a strip club afterwards. Later, the couple told the police that they had been planning to kill someone together as a couple for some time, thinking that it would bring them closer and strengthen their relationship. They had tried to kill a few times before, but Troy was the first person to actually show up after they placed an ad. After the murder, Miranda and Elytte continued their lives normally. She started posting happy updates on Facebook. On November 19, she posted a picture of her new wedding ring. Her posts were cheerful and about the happy holidays.

During that time, the Sunbury police were investigating the murder of Troy. There were many leads to follow. Some texts messages on the victim's phone led them to Miranda. On December 3, 2013, Miranda was arrested. Elytte was arrested a few days later, after surveillance footage showed him buying cleaning supplies with her after the murder. Social services immediately took her baby away and gave custody to Miranda's father, who is fighting for custody against Miranda's uncle Arlin.

Initially, prosecutors indicated they would seek a death penalty sentence for the couple. But in August of 2014, both Miranda and Elytte pleaded guilty to second-degree murder charges. They face mandatory life sentences without the possibility of parole, and they will both be sentenced on September 18, 2014, the day this book publishes. Miranda still claims that she actually committed more than twenty murders in her lifetime. Miranda says that she is ready to show the FBI and the authorities where the dumped bodies are, but tells them they will find only parts of the victims. According to her claims, some parts are dumped in Mexico Beach in Florida where she had worked as a go-go dancer when she was 15; other parts are dumped in Big Lake, Alaska; and one body was dumped at the Interstate 95 near Raleigh in North Carolina. However, any truth behind Miranda's claims has yet to be proven.

Chapter 29: Richard Beasley

Over the years, Craigslist has been a useful tool to help people find work. But if a person responding to an ad is not careful, he or she can end up a victim.

Richard Beasley was born in the year 1959. His mother, who worked at a local high school, and his stepfather, raised him in Akron, Ohio. As an adult, he married once and had a daughter named Tonya. He was working as a mechanist, but spent many years in and out of prison. Between 1985 and 1990, he was in a Texas prison on burglary charges. He spent 1996 to 2003 in another prison for a firearms crime. A few years after getting out of prison, Richard was hit by a dump truck. He suffered injuries on the chest, head, and spine. After that accident, he stopped his steady work and started taking pills for his back and neck pains. He also began to claim that he had found God and started spending time at the local church. Richard did not smoke, nor did he drink, and he seemed to be a good and nice man who did not lose his temper.

During this time, the Rafferty family was living in the same neighborhood as Richard. Michael, the father, knew Richard from a local motorcycle circuit. Richard became a close friend of the family—so much so that he took care of Michael's son, Brogan, and often took the eight-year-old boy to church with him. For eight years, Richard took Brogan to church every Sunday, sometimes taking along his daughter Tonya and Brogan's half-sister, Rayna. Brogan had a tough childhood. His mother was a drug addict and was hardly around. His father, Michael, was always working and when he was at home he would easily lose his temper; he was hard on his children. That is why Brogan saw a father figure in Richard.

In 2009, Richard founded a halfway home hoping to provide support for runaways, addicts, and prostitutes. He often picked these people up from the streets at night and let them stay at his house. One woman, Amy Saller, was living on and off in that house between 2009 and 2011. She later recalled that Richard had a dark side.

She stated that he claimed to want to help the girls get off the streets and get back on track, but once they were in the house he acted as their pimp, featuring their services on the internet. He could do anything to keep them in the house, and that included giving them drugs. Although he was never violent, Amy was afraid of Richard.

In February 2011, Richard was arrested on drug charges. While in jail, authorities were preparing prostitution charges against him. In July, Richard was released on bond, but when he didn't check with his parole officer, a warrant was issued for his arrest. Richard needed to disappear and had an idea on how to do just that. He told Brogan that he would need his help.

Richard was searching for a new identity. At a homeless refuge home, he looked for a person that resembled him. Soon he found the perfect match: fifty-six-year-old Ralph Geiger. To lure him, he would present a great job opportunity of being a concierge of a farm. Ralph was searching for work and had spent his early years on a farm, so he jumped at the opportunity. It is not clear if

Brogan knew that Richard would kill Ralph. On August 9, Richard and Brogan drove Ralph to a secluded area in the woods, where Richard shot him in the back of his head using a pistol.

Brogan didn't inform anyone about the murder of Geiger, but on August 16, 2011, he described it in the form of a poem that was discovered on his computer's hard drive. The poem was titled "Midnight Shift" and read:

We took him out to the woods on a
humid summer's night.
I walked in front of them.
They were going back to the car.
I did'nt turn around.
The loud crack echoed and I did'nt
hear the thud.
The two of us went back to the car
for the shovels.
He was still there when we returned.
He threw the clothes in a garbage
bag along with the personal items.
I dug the hole.
It reached my waist when I was in

it, maybe four feet wide.
We put him in with difficulty,
they call them stiffs for a reason.
We showered him with lime like a
Satanic baptism
it was like we were excommunicating
him from the world
I thought there would be extra dirt,
he was'nt a small man.
There wasint. I don't know how.
We drove out of there discarding
evidence as we went
felt terrible until I threw up
in the gas station bathroom where
I was supposed to throw away the bullets
and shell.
I emptied myself of my guilt, with
my dinner, but not for long.
When I got home, ' took a shower hotter than
hell itsself.
prayed like hell that night.

Brogan was a changed teen after that night. He started drinking heavily and wishing he would die, even thinking about wrecking his car. But still, he didn't tell anyone about the murder. He stayed alone in his room and waited for Richard to contact him. In the meantime, Richard was assuming the life of Ralph Geiger. He colored his hair, rented a room, and found a job as a quality inspection officer. However, his back was still hurting and he was still on prescribed painkillers, so the job didn't last long. Richard was afraid that he would get caught and he needed money. That is when he had another idea for income.

Richard must have felt invincible when no one suspected that he had committed a murder, so he thought he would go on killing and stealing from his victims. However, he needed to find his victims outside shelters so they would have something of value to be stolen. To cover for the sudden influx of income he was expecting, Richard decided to pretend that had been bidding on abandoned storage units that contained valuables, following the reality TV show *Storage Wars*. Then he posted a Craigslist advertisement to lure middle aged white males. The ad read:

Wanted: Caretaker For Farm. Simply watch over a 688 acre patch of hilly farm-

land and feed a few cows, you get 300 a week and a nice 2 bedroom trailer, someone older and single preferred but will consider all, relocation a must, you must have a clean record and be trustworthy—this is a permanent position, the farm is used mainly as a hunting preserve, is overrun with game, has a stocked 3 acre pond, but some beef cattle will be kept, nearest neighbor is a mile away, the place is secluded and beautiful, it will be a real get away for the right person, job of a lifetime—if you are ready to relocate please contact asap, position will not stay open.

Hundreds of applicants contacted Richard, who used the name Jack, for the job. However, 'Jack' had a certain criteria: he needed someone single or divorced, someone who would not be missed, not very large, and someone who had some valuables and would relocate without hesitation. The first man to match this criteria was David Pauley, a fifty-one-year-old divorced man who lived with his older brother and his wife in Norfolk, Virginia. David had been married to his high school sweetheart, and had adopted her son, Wade, but they divorced in 2009. After 2003, David quit his job at Randolph-Bundy and had bounced from one job to another, never finding anything stable. When he saw the ad in October 2011, David was extremely excited.

The job was in Ohio, where his best friend, Chris Maul, had moved some years ago. David and Chris talked everyday using their Nextel walkie-talkies. David and 'Jack' exchanged a few emails, and David was informed that he made it to the narrow list of three final candidates. He was so excited when he received a call from Jack saying that he had been accepted for the job. David called first his friend, Chris, and then his twin sister, Deb, who lived in Maine. They were both happy for him. Nobody knew the horrible fate that was waiting for David. October 22 was the last time David had contacted Chris and Deb before meeting his soon to be employer. The two became worried when they received no news from David for several days, so they decided to call 'Jack,' who told them that everything was fine and that David had left with a list of chores. When still David didn't call, Chris called 'Jack' again, and was told that David had left the farm in pursuit of another job with some guy in Pennsylvania. Chris and Deb found this odd—they didn't think he would leave without telling them about it. What they didn't know is that 'Jack' had already murdered David and sold all his possessions, news that would hit David's family hard later on.

After killing David, Richard was already luring another victim. On October 9, forty-eight-year-old Scott Davis answered the ad placed by Richard as 'Jack.' One month later, after being accepted for the job, Scott was sitting in the backseat of the white Buick LeSabre driven by Brogan and his uncle 'Jack,' on the way to the farm. Scott had left his girlfriend in South Carolina after telling her about his new job. He had packed up his belongings and hitched his Harley-Davidson to the back of his truck in a trailer. As they drove through the road that would lead them to the farm, Scott saw the signal on his phone get weaker until it disappeared. Then Jack asked his nephew to pull over where they haunted their last deer, claiming there was some equipment they had left behind. Earlier, Jack had explained to Scott that the road needed some fixing before they could bring up his trailer up to the farm. As they walked up the road, Scott followed. Jack claimed that he had lost his way and asked Scott to turn around and head back. As Scott turned, he heard a click followed by the word, "fuck." He turned to face Jack and saw him pointing a gun at him. Jack fired but hit Scott in the right elbow. Scott turned and tried to escape. He ran deeper into the woods as the shots followed, but missed. Scott was losing blood. After waiting hours until it was clear, he walked back up to the road searching for help. He was able to reach the house of Jeff Schockling and asked him to call 911. The Sheriff, Stephen Hannum, arrived to the house about fifteen minutes later. His first impression was that Scott was involved in a drug deal gone wrong. Scott told the Sheriff that his truck and trailer were parked at the Food Center Emporium parking lot where 'Jack' had suggested that he park them until the road was clear. When he found them, the Sheriff began to realize that Scott was actually a victim.

In the meantime, Deb, David's twin sister, was trying to find an explanation for the disappearance of her brother. She called a number of motels or rental places that David might have stayed in, but nothing was helpful. On November 11, Deb remembered that David had mentioned that farm was located in a town named Cambridge. She looked up the name online and found an article in the local paper, *The Daily Jeffersonian,* dated November 8. It was about a man who was lured with a job promise then he was shot. Deb paid attention to one specific detail: the farm was supposedly comprised of 688 acres. Deb called the Sheriff immediately. The Sheriff initially had difficulty believing Scott's story, but when he received a call from Deb, he put more effort into unveiling the truth behind this mystery. An FBI cybercrimes specialist was called in for help in tracing the Craigslist ad. In addition, a crew with dogs was sent to search the woods where Scott was shot. It only took them a few hours to find David's body. They knew they were dealing with a serial killer, especially after they found an empty grave, which was meant for Scott.

After Scott had gotten away, Richard did not stop his killings. By November 13, he had already found his next victim. Richard and Brogan met up with Timothy Kern, a forty-seven-year-old divorced man. Timothy had two children who were the center of his life. Not one day would go by without him contacting his teenage boys, Zachary and Nicholas. When he met Richard, Timothy had just lost his street cleaning job. He was very excited to accept the job from Richard, but sad he would be two hours away from his children.

When he met up with Richard and Brogan, he didn't bring with him anything of value; instead he had given everything valuable to his sons. Brogan later recounted that he had felt pity for the man who clearly loved his sons so much and that he was helping Richard kill Timothy for no reason. Timothy described himself as single (he and his wife had divorced in 1997) and ready to relocate anytime, but he didn't mention his sons. Instead of getting a job, Timothy was taken to an abandoned area behind an empty mall. His grave was already dug up. Richard shot Timothy five times before he died. His sons were devastated when they learned the news that their father had been murdered.

Less than one week after they found David's body, investigators were able to identify the killer as a local man, Richard Beasley. They were also able to trace the IP address from which the ad was sent from to the house of Joe Bais, whom Richard rented a room from under the name of Ralph Greiger, his first victim. Joe helped the investigators trace a phone call he made to Richard who left to rent a room at another house in Akron. They were also able to track down the teenager who was helping Richard with the killings. They arrested Brogan after searching his house and interviewing his school's principal. After that, Richard was also arrested.

During the trial in 2013, Richard's mother was called to the stand. She said that Richard had been physically abused by his stepfather and sexually abused by some of the neighborhood's youngsters. A psychologist testified that Richard suffered from depression and low self-esteem, possibly because of the abuse he suffered from as a child. Since Brogan was sixteen at the time of crimes, there was no possibility for a death penalty sentence; instead he was sentenced to life imprisonment. During Richard's trial, the defense tried to bring up Brogan's case and the life in prison sentence so that the jury would consider that in their conviction, but the prosecutors highlighted the fact that the death penalty for Brogan was out of question. In the end, the jury convicted Richard and suggested the death penalty. The judge could have sentenced him to life imprisonment, but instead he handed him a death sentence. Richard passed on the opportunity to speak with the judge before receiving his sentence, which was read in the presence of the victim's families.

After hearing the sentence, Richard requested to speak with the judge but was told that his chance had passed. He insisted that he didn't kill anyone and that the ruling will be overturned. Richard believes his conviction will be overturned and he will be found innocent at a retrial.

There has been a speculation that there was a sexual relationship between Richard and Brogan, which may indicate why Brogan was so loyal to Richard until the end. Brogan has denied all of these claims and stated that he had looked up to Richard like a father but at the same time he was afraid that Richard would hurt his family if he had told anyone about the murders.

Chapter 30: Richard Alden Samuel McCroskey III

In 2009, Richard "Sammy" McCroskey had rather interesting career aspirations. Twenty-year-old McCroskey went by the stage names 'Lil Demon Dog' and 'Syko Sam,' and dreamed of making headlines as a big time 'horrorcore' rapper. Horrorcore is a type of 'gangsta rap' that uses particularly violent and gory lyrics and supernatural themes. McCroskey lived in California and, according to reports, was kind of a loner. With his red hair and slightly overweight frame, he had always been picked on in school. As a result, he spent much of his teenage years in isolation on his computer. It is there where he discovered his love for horrorcore lyrics and started his own amateur career as a rapper. His MySpace profile was peppered with videos and lyrics of his own, often detailing how much he enjoyed killing. In one of his songs, he raps, "You're not the first, just to let you know. I've killed many people and I kill them real slow. It's the best kind of feeling, watching their last breath. Stabbing and stabbing till there's nothing left."

One of those people he met online was Emma Niederbrok, a sixteen-year-old from Farmville, Virginia, who went by the online persona 'Ragdoll.' Emma's parents were going through a divorce when she met 'Syko Sam' in an online community dedicated to horrorcore music. Despite living on opposite sides of the country and never having met in person, Emma and McCroskey hit it off and quickly became an item. The two spent hours each day communicating online and talking on the phone, commiserating about the agonies of teenage life and their love for violent, gory music.

After dating online for nearly a year, on Sunday, September 6, 2009, McCroskey flew from California to Virginia to finally meet Emma in person. The two had been looking forward to the trip for weeks. They planned to drive to Michigan to attend the 'Strictly for the Wicked' concert, a music festival featuring horrorcore bands with macabre names like Dismembered Fetus and

Phrozen Body Boy. The couple, along with Emma's friend, Melanie Wells, and Emma's parents, Debra Kelley (a university professor who taught sociology and criminal justice) and Mark Niederbrok (a pastor at the local Presbyterian church), who had been separated for almost nine months at this point, all drove to the concert together. While Emma's parents did not approve of the type of music she was listening to, they mostly considered it to be a phase their teenager was going through and volunteered to take the group to the concert largely to keep an eye on them.

At some point during the concert, it is believed that McCroskey and Emma got into an argument of sorts, purportedly over text messages she may have sent to another friend. It is believed McCroskey stewed in his anger about this argument during the long drive back to Virginia. Once they arrived back at Debra Kelley's home, Mark Niederbrok returned to his home as well. Emma, Melanie, and McCroskey all stayed the night with Debra being the only parent in the house. That night, McCroskey drank alcohol, smoked marijuana, and took painkillers, all the while becoming more and more upset with how things had turned out with Emma. Police believe after spending a year talking to her online, he had imagined things going much differently for them when they finally met.

The timeline after returning home from the concert is a little unclear. What is known is that the girls last logged into their respective MySpace accounts on Monday, September 14. The next day, McCroskey called his family back in California and left them a message ending with, "I love you guys," something extremely out of character. In fact, this comment led his sister to suspect something was terribly wrong.

Two days later, Melanie's mother contacted the police after not being able to reach her daughter for several days. The police made a courtesy call to Debra Kelley's residence to check on Melanie's welfare, where McCroskey answered the door. He calmly told police that Melanie and Emma were at the movies. Thinking everything seemed normal, the police took his word for it. This same day, Emma's father, Mark, stopped in at his estranged wife's house before leaving for a meeting in Richmond. He was never seen alive again.

McCroskey later stole Mark's car, and left the residence. Around 4:00 a.m. on Friday, September 18, he wrecked the car. Police arrived at the scene and ticketed him for driving without a license. Since the car wasn't reported stolen, they simply gave the twenty-year-old a ticket and left the scene. A tow-truck driver was called for the vehicle and the driver later reported that he drove McCroskey to a convenience store about four miles away. He claimed that the stench coming off McCroskey's clothes during the ride was so pungent and disgusting, he had almost gagged.

Approximately twelve hours later, after Melanie's mother called police again and begged them to conduct another welfare check on the home, police could tell something was wrong when they approached the house. This time, they could smell the decomposing bodies as they walked up the driveway. Inside the home, they found the bodies of Emma, Melanie, Debra, and Mark. They had been bludgeoned beyond recognition with a ball-peen hammer and a wood-splitting maul. It is believed that McCroskey murdered Emma, Melanie, and Debra sometime on Monday and remained in the residence with the bodies until Mark showed up on Thursday, when he killed him as well and fled the scene in the victim's vehicle.

The medical examiner believes he killed Melanie first, while she slept on a couch in the downstairs den. He then moved upstairs, where he murdered Emma's mother in her bedroom as she slept. Finally, he walked back downstairs, where he killed Emma in a similar manner. According to the medical examiner, none of the first three victims woke up during the attacks. They did not have any sort of defensive wounds. When Mark arrived at the house a few days later, McCroskey attacked him in the living room with the same weapons. He then moved Mark and Melanie's bodies into Emma's room and attempted to clean up the downstairs.

Court documents state that at some point,

McCroskey recorded himself on a digital camera, confessing to his crimes and contemplating suicide.

One of McCroskey's friends contacted the police on Friday after getting an alarming message from him claiming he had "killed everyone." After police discovered the bodies, they began searching for McCroskey, realizing they had just been in contact with him twelve hours earlier and had let an alleged murderer go. They learned he had called a cab from the convenience store where the tow-truck driver had dropped him off and finally located McCroskey at the Richmond International Airport. According to police, he didn't seem too surprised when they apprehended him and brought him down to the station.

He was initially charged with first-degree murder, robbery, and grand larceny. His charges were later increased to a total of six counts of capital murder. He was put on suicide watch while he awaited his trial. When police asked him why he had murdered them, he told them, "Jesus told me to do it."

In September of 2010, McCroskey pleaded guilty to his crimes. Some of Debra's students started an online petition asking prosecutors to take the death penalty off the table. They claimed Debra was vehemently against capital punishment and sentencing McCroskey to death would only serve to dishonor her beliefs. He was ultimately sentenced to life in prison and waived his right to file an appeal.

In memory of Debra Kelley and the three other victims, students at Longwood University planted holly trees on campus. Residents of the small town of Farmville, Virginia expressed shock and sorrow over the senseless killings. Many of the students came together after the murders to talk about the dangers of meeting friends online. Some of Debra Kelley's students even deactivated their MySpace profiles soon after the murders.

Chapter 31: William Francis Melchert-Dinkel

With all the services the internet has made available, predators don't even need to meet their victims face to face anymore in order to cause them harm. Yet, somehow people feel safer sharing intimate details of their lives with a stranger, not knowing if the person they are talking to has a hidden dark agenda. Unfortunately, many have been the victims of the sick fantasies and addictions of others.

William Francis Melchert-Dinkel was born on July 20, 1962 in Faribault, Minnesota. As an adult, he married and had two teenage daughters. Others described him as a loving, caring churchgoer. However, even his own wife knew nothing about his second darker self and suicide fetish.

William started his career as a licensed practical nurse. However, his records were tarnished with disciplinary actions. In 1994, while working in a medical facility, he was giving medications to patients without noting them in the patients' charts; he also did not report medical errors; and did not document one patient's condition or update the physician about the case, an action which resulted in the death of that patient. William was officially reprimanded. In 1996, he worked in a hospital where he was also given a warning because of his lack of nursing care and his unsafe decisions. Two years later, in 1998, the Minnesota Board of Nursing placed restrictions on his license because there was evidence of him mistreating patients for four years. These restrictions remained active until 2003. At one point in his career, William worked in a retirement home but was fired because he allegedly abused two of the residents.

The nursing board determined that William was not practicing safe medicine, nor was he able to follow simple instructions or retain information. In the report made, there was a mention of problems he had at home, and also a mention of his diagnosis of Adjustment Reaction with Anxiety and Attention Deficit Hyperactivity Disorder.

William began visiting suicide chat

rooms as a part of his double life to prey on vulnerable people and encourage them to commit suicide in front of him on the webcam. He pretended to be a young female nurse in her twenties who compassionately chatted with depressed people. Later, William admitted that he had tried to convince at least twenty people (although the number could be much higher) to kill themselves, entered into a suicide pact with ten of them, of which he believed five actually committed suicide. He did all of this for (in his own words) "the thrill of the chase." This went on for several years. Included in the group of five people who were thought to have committed suicide after William's encouragement are Mark Drybrough of the United Kingdom and Nadia Kajouji of Canada.

Thirty-two-year-old Mark Drybrough of Coventry, England, was an IT technician who had been suffering from depression for several years. His condition started after he had contracted a glandular fever (also known as infectious mononucleosis). When he committed suicide in June 2005, his family was shocked. They knew about his condition, but they did not know that he was suicidal; it was just not like him. Later, they would find out that on the morning of the day in which he killed himself, Mark had been communicating with a female nurse who was using the nickname 'Li Dao.' Minutes before Mark hanged himself from a ladder in an upstairs bedroom, he received a message from Li Dao asking, "Are you all right?" After reading through two months of chat history between Mark and 'Li Dao,' they discovered that the two had made a suicide pact.

Around November of 2006, Celia Bay, a sixty-four-year-old British schoolteacher and grandmother who lived in Maiden Bradley, Wiltshire, England, had received word that a teenage friend of the family had made a suicide pact with a female nurse. The nurse was using the name 'Li Dao.' Celia was able to convince the girl to postpone her suicide plans (four hours before the suicide) in order to give her more time to investigate. Thanks to Celia, that girl is still alive. However, some hard work was waiting for Celia. She had heard about the suicide of Mark

Drybrough and made the connection between his case and the teenage girl's case due to the use of the same nickname 'Li Dao.' Further investigation led her into discovering that the same person was using other nicknames such as 'Falcon Girl' and 'Cami D.' As she contacted other people, she also found out that this individual had entered into suicide pacts with other people as well, encouraging them to kill themselves in front of the webcam. Each time, 'Li Dao's' webcam always encountered technical problems, and no one had ever seen her face. Celia posted warnings about that person on the chat websites. After spending months trying to collect evidence about the case, she went to the local authorities, who refused to initiate an investigation. Celia realized she was fighting this battle on her own, so she decided to get help elsewhere.

Celia got help from thirty-seven-year-old Katherine Lowe, an unemployed mother of two living in Wolver Hampton. Around January 2008, Kat and Celia decided to catch this individual in the act. At the same time, 'Falcon Girl' (or 'Li Dao' or 'Cami D') was

247

already claiming another victim.

Eighteen-year-old Nadia Kajouji was an attractive student in the Carleton University in Ottawa, Ontario. She was studying public affairs and policy. It was her first year and she was having trouble adjusting to the university life. On March 9, 2008, Nadia disappeared. That Sunday was the last day her roommates had seen her. Her family, fearing that Nadia was involved in a foul play, urged the police to conduct search, which they did. Nadia's belongings were all found in her room, including her driver's license and her wallet, indicating she did not run away. On her computer, the police discovered Nadia had been visiting online chat rooms devoted to suicide. Believing that Nadia would not kill herself, the family traveled to Ottawa, crossing more than 300 miles, to help with search. They even announced a reward of $50,000 for her safe return home. The family knew that she was going through some hard times, but she was not suicidal. Just like Mark's family before, Nadia's family was wrong. On April 19, 2008, someone found the body of a woman on a rock on the area of the Rideau River, which runs behind the Saint Paul University, a few kilometers away from the Carleton University. The body was identified as Nadia's, and it was ruled as a suicide since there was no evidence of any foul play.

Meanwhile, Celia Bay and Katherine Lowe continued their investigation in full force. Katherine had been contacting 'Falcon Girl' and gained her trust. The individual told Katherine that she was a nurse working in an emergency room in a United States hospital, and claimed that she had experience and could give advice about the best way for a person to commit suicide. 'Falcon Girl' even claimed that she had watched a man kill himself some years earlier. The man was not identified, but 'Falcon Girl' claimed that he was from Birmingham, England. 'Falcon Girl' assured Katherine that she would go with the suicide pact this time, although other times she didn't. According to their chat log, these are some of the messages they they exchanged:

- *"The four people you think hanged them-*

selves, did they do it while you were online?" (said by Katherine)
- *"No, just one."* (said by 'Falcon Girl')
- *"When the guy in Birmingham went, why did you not go, too?"* (said by Katherine)
- *"I was put on a new drug [to] see if I could get better"* (said by 'Falcon Girl')
- *"I am scared"* (said by Katherine)
- *"I know. I agreed to help you 'cause we both know each of us is sincere about needing to die. That is why I agreed to watch/help you if [you] needed it."* (said by 'Falcon Girl')
- *"I have tried cutting my wrists"* (said by Katherine)
- *"That is why I really suggested the rope 'cause it's so much more dependable."* (said by 'Falcon Girl')

Later, 'Falcon Girl' sent a picture of a female to Katherine. However, the picture's filename was the name of a male. Katherine began suspecting that she was speaking to a totally different person. Moreover, in her chats with other members of the groups, she learned that the same individual was using different names, including 'Li Dao' and 'Cami D.' The members were able to figure this out because of the individual's choice of words, topics, and the way the three nicknames expressed things—instead of offering support, 'Falcon Girl' (and her other aliases) encouraged people to actually commit suicide. Katherine was lucky enough to convince 'Falcon Girl' to use the webcam. She saw a man and was able to take a picture of him with her mobile phone. At last, Katherine had enough information to trace this person's IP address to the suburbs of St. Paul, Minnesota.

Celia and Katherine took the information they collected, including a transcript of the chats between Katherine and 'Falcon Girl,' to the police in the United Kingdom, who rejected the case. They also sent the information to the FBI, who also rejected the case, due to jurisdictional issues that prevented them from launching an investigation. However, these two women along with

Mark's mother, Mrs. Drybrough, did not give up. Finally, the police department of St. Paul, Minnesota, agreed to take the case after they reviewed all the evidence collected by the women. The true identity and home address of 'Falcon Girl' was discovered—it was William Francis Melchert-Dinkel.

It is not known exactly how many people William convinced to commit suicide. He could have contacted hundreds of people over several years. He always pushed them to carry out with their suicidal plans. He also suggested ways in which they could do it. Thanks to the efforts carried out by the three women in the United Kingdom, The link between the suicides of Mark Drybrough and Nadia Kajouji was made to William Melchert-Dinkel. It was discovered that before her death, Nadia was contacting William in the suicide chat rooms, under the name 'Cami D.' The police also discovered that William had entered into many suicide pacts with people from all over the world. William had to be hospitalized after questioning because of his behavior. He told the nurses in the hospital that he was addicted to

252

the chat rooms where he could meet suicidal people and that he had encouraged many to kill themselves.

On February 5, the nursing board suspended William's license. He was seen as a risk to the lives of others. After a few months, his nursing license was revoked entirely.

On April 30, 2010, William was charged with encouraging Mark Drybrough to commit suicide in 2005, and Nadia Kajouji in 2008. It was a controversial case because William didn't physically assist with the suicide of these people, he only encouraged them to kill themselves verbally; he was practicing his freedom of speech. However, William was convicted on March 15, 2011 under a rarely used Minnesota law, forbidding individuals from advising and encouraging other people to commit suicide, a charge that could have resulted in fifteen years in prison and a $30,000 fine. The court ordered William to stay off the internet during his trial. On May 4, 2011, William was sentenced to just 360 days in jail. On July 27 2012, the Minnesota Court of Appeals affirmed his sentence. In early 2014, the State Supreme Court ruled that anyone advising or encouraging suicide is protected under the First Amendment right of free speech. His conviction was reversed and the case was sent to the lower court to determine the outcome. At the time this book went to press, closing arguments had been heard and William was waiting to hear Rice Co. District Court Judge Tom Neuville's ruling.

Chapter 32: Derek Medina

Social media monsters don't just use the internet to locate and lure their victims—some of them have used social media to actually confess.

Derek Medina, a six-foot-two, 200-pound property management supervisor living in Miami, Florida posted many of his life's activities on social media. He often posted photos and videos of himself working out and engaging in his hobbies, such as kick boxing and sailing. He was also a writer and published six self-help eBooks detailing the importance of communication to a successful marriage. He promoted the books on his website and Facebook page. One of those books was titled, *How I Saved Someone's Life and Marriage and Family Problems Thru Communication.*

Derek married Jennifer Alfonso in 2010. The couple actually divorced in February 2012, but remarried just three months later. Neighbors in the condominium complex where the couple lived with their daughter found him to be polite, but odd. He often walked around the complex, patrolling the area, telling anyone who would listen that he was on patrol for the neighborhood watch. He also told others that he had a concealed weapon permit and carried a gun at all times.

On August 8, 2013, Derek's Facebook friends were shocked to read a rambling post from him at 11:11 in the morning: "Im [sic] going to prison or death sentence for killing my wife love you guys, miss you guys takecare [sic] Facebook people you will see me in the news." He went on attempting to justify his actions: "my wife was punching me and I am not going to stand anymore with the abuse so I did what I did I hope u [sic] understand me." Minutes later, he posted a photo of Jennifer's body on the kitchen floor of their home. She was on her back with her legs bent awkwardly underneath her at her sides. Her arms splayed out away from her body and one of them appeared to be covered in blood. Jennifer's chin rested on her chest and her head was tilted at an unnatural angle. Along with the photo,

Derek typed, "RIP Jennifer Alfonso."

To the horror of everyone who knew Jennifer, the gruesome photo and Facebook post remained live on the site for more than five hours, where it was shared over 170 times. Dubbed the "Facebook killer," Derek Medina's story made headlines almost instantly. Facebook finally took action after receiving reports from Jennifer's friends and family. They removed the disturbing image and posts and contacted law enforcement at that time.

According to Derek, the two had gotten into an argument in their upstairs bedroom. When Derek pointed a gun at her, Jennifer left the room. She then turned around and told him she was leaving him. Derek followed her down the stairs where he said she began punching him. He told officers he went back upstairs to retrieve his gun and by the time he got back to the kitchen, Jennifer had grabbed a knife. Derek claimed he successfully snatched the knife out of Jennifer's clutches and put it back in a drawer when she began to punch him again. That's when he shot her six times, killing her.

He then snapped a picture of his dead wife's body, posted the image to Facebook, changed his clothes, and drove himself to the South Miami Police Department, where he turned himself in. When police arrived at the scene, they found Jennifer's body in the kitchen, where he had left it. Her ten-year-old daughter from a previous relationship was also in the residence, hiding upstairs wrapped in a blanket. She was unharmed.

Derek pleaded not guilty to second-degree murder charges. Surveillance footage from the couple's home released later showed the moments leading up to the murder. While the video doesn't clearly show the murder take place, the two can be seen arguing. Derek leaves the room briefly before returning. Gunpowder can be seen in the video when the gun is fired. He then calmly snaps a picture of her corpse before walking back upstairs to change clothes before leaving.

The autopsy report concluded that Jennifer was shot multiple times in her left forearm, indicating she had been trying to shield herself from the gunfire. The bullets traveled through her body in a downward trajectory, suggesting she had been cowering on the floor in front of him with her arms up in a protective manner. This completely contradicted what Derek had told police about Jennifer being the aggressor.

In December of 2013, prosecutors increased the charges to first-degree murder in light of those autopsy results. Derek continued to maintain his actions were in self-defense and pleaded not guilty. In January, his defense team requested to test the victim's tissue samples for traces of a drug called Alpha PVP, more commonly known as "bath salts," known to cause paranoia, panic, and agitation. The defense team claimed to have found a batch of pills that did not belong in a jar of garlic supplements in the couple's kitchen. The surveillance video released by police shows Jennifer reach into the cabinet where the bottle was found approximately eleven hours before the murder. In May 2014, the medical examiner released his findings—there were no drugs in Jennifer's system at all.

Investigators claim that Derek told others

that he would kill Jennifer if she ever cheated on him or tried to leave him. They insist he was the aggressor in the situation. His trial is set to start on October 14, 2014. While he is facing first-degree murder charges, the Miami-Dade State Attorney's Office has announced that they will not be seeking the death penalty in this case.

Chapter 33: Brady Oestrike

Thirty-one-year-old Brady Oestrike's friends knew him as a guy who enjoyed medieval fare and going to Renaissance festivals. According to his Facebook page, he was highly religious and even studied at the Montana Wilderness School of the Bible. He once took a trip with his church group to help build a school and hospital in the Dominican Republic. He worked as a lineman, repairing power lines for a local electric company in Wyoming, Michigan. He was engaged to be married at some point, but when his fiancée broke off the engagement in 2013, friends claim he fell into a serious depression. To many who knew him, he was a generous, kind, and normal guy.

In April of 2014, Brady allegedly entered a bar he frequented in Eastown, Michigan and told several people he had a woman tied up in his home. He claimed to have met a woman on Craigslist, zipped her into a suitcase, and took her home in the trunk of his car. He then allegedly left her tied up in his home while he went to the bar. Alarmed, the bar staff called police and relayed the story to them. When police investigated further, they discovered that the woman was fine and had simply been participating in some role-playing with Brady. Since no crime had been committed, investigators closed the case.

Three months later, Brady responded to a Craigslist ad placed by an eighteen-year-old named Brooke Slocum and her twenty-five-year-old boyfriend, Charlie Oppenneer. Brooke was eight months pregnant with her first child. Sources close to the investigation claim Brooke and Charlie described they were looking for a sexual partner in exchange for money. In part, the post allegedly read, "Hello! A little about me: I am 18, 5'3" about 120lbs now and still growing (I happen to be 8 months pregnant with a beautiful white/Korean baby girl), I am white and petite, short brown hair and green eyes… father of my child and I are sort of involved in this weird open relationship." Brooke's roommate later told the media that the couple often met up with people who responded to their ads on Craigslist. Charlie always accompanied Brooke on these meet-ups, and sometimes he would even participate in the sex acts.

Brooke's father later spoke out to the media. He claimed he was aware of his daughter's dangerous habit of meeting up with strangers and he had tried to discourage her from continuing with such behavior. But he said she was in love with Charlie and easily manipulated by him. The two had briefly broken up in early July and Brooke was planning on moving in with her mother. Instead, she made amends with her boyfriend and the two continued seeking out potential sex clients on Craigslist.

Charlie and Brooke arranged to meet Brady at Gezon Park on July 12, 2014. Four days later, police found Charlie's body in a wooded area after they were alerted to an abandoned vehicle. His head had been removed and was missing. The medical examiner later determined that Charlie was dead before his head was removed, but without locating the head, the cause of death is still unknown. At the time of this writing, his head was still missing.

It wasn't long before police realized that Charlie's pregnant girlfriend was missing too. Investigators searched their apartment and discovered the emails Brooke had exchanged with Brady about the sexual meetup. Police began watching Brady's home while they waited for a search warrant to search his residence. They had requested a SWAT team to assist with the search because they believed he was in possession of assault weapons. Around 9:15 on Thursday night, July 17, Brady got into his vehicle and sped off. A high-speed chase ensued, but ended when Brady crashed his vehicle. Police found him dead in the front seat with a self-inflicted gunshot wound to the head. When they opened the trunk to his car, they found the body of Brooke Slocum. She had been strangled to death. Her unborn child, a girl she had planned on naming Audi Lynn, never had a chance to live. A medical examiner determined her death was more recent than Charlie's.

Police then entered Brady's home, which they later described to the media as a "hellish environment." They removed firearms, ammunition, and medieval weapons and knives from the residence. Apparently, Brady had kept Brook captive in the residence for five days, enslaved in medieval restraints he had in his home.

After his death, several of Brady's friends spoke with the media. One of them was twenty-three-year-old Brittany Zemaitis. She claimed that Brady had sunk into a deep depression after his fiancée broke of their engagement. He allegedly spoke about suicide and once told her that he was a dangerous person. She said he had once told her wished he could live in an era where he could kill people with his bare hands.

Brady's former roommate also spoke with the media after the brutal slayings. Rachel Morris claimed she wasn't surprised by his actions. She claimed his depression had begun to escalate and she knew he was having bad dreams and writing dark poetry. She moved out of the home in 2012 when he warned her he was having dark thoughts about killing her. Rachel told the media she urged Brady to speak to a mental health professional and he told her he believed he was suffering from schizophrenia but he was terrified of losing his job. "I think in the end," she said, "the fears and the thoughts that he was having won—and Brady didn't."

At the time of this writing, investigators were comparing notes with other police departments in Michigan and working to determine if Brady Oestrike might be connected with any other crimes, including that of the disappearance of Jessica Heeringa, a night clerk at an Exxon gas station in Grand Rapids who mysteriously disappeared on April 26, 2013.

Chapter 34: How Law Enforcement Uses Social Media to Hunt Criminals

While this book has mainly focused on the negative aspects of social media, there is a positive side that we haven't yet discussed. There is no doubt, whatsoever, that law enforcement agencies are using social media to solve various crimes in the world.

It has been known that criminals are using the social networks regularly to boast about their crimes. They interact with their friends about how they plotted their crimes. Some have gone so far as to upload images and videos incriminating themselves, not realizing that the police would actually see them. What they don't realize is that in many cases, a Facebook friend in the same community could actually be a paid confidential informant. RJ Parker once said in an interview, "man is a social animal and perhaps a criminal man is more so." Criminals who cannot hold back from online bragging are a big blessing to both the police department and prosecutors all over the world.

The Center for Social Media at the International Association of Chiefs of Police (IACP) reported that police departments first ventured out into the social networking channels by tapping into MySpace around 2005, which then spread to Facebook and grew from there.

Private investigators attached to credit bureaus have also become socially sophisticated after using LinkedIn, Twitter, and Facebook to prove frauds after confirming the identities of suspects. Sometimes their efforts are as plain as checking photographs but they can even identify people by the way they post their status updates—they can often determine whether people are natives of the region or from other states or countries by checking the grammar and colloquial language they use on social media.

How has social media become a helpful instrument in tracking criminals?
Every one of us leaves some kind of clues concerning our lives all over the social media channels, just like fingerprints. Social media has changed the ways business is

conducted on a professional range from Facebook to Twitter and from LinkedIn to MySpace, Flickr, and YouTube. Officers of law enforcement agencies have been able to find unique methods to use the social networking channels to hire informants and to solve crimes. Social networking has proven to be the ideal partner in preventing and solving crimes. This also includes blogs, blog comments, chat rooms, forums, and news article comments. Big Brother is watching them all for particular key words in a very sophisticated program that is shared internationally.

Today, with the help of social media, many investigation agencies are able to gain new insights into how crimes were committed in their communities, counties, and states. There is no denying the fact that Facebook and Twitter are definitely helping these agencies to catch criminals. Police are now in a position to get tipped off from friends of the suspects once a particular suspect starts posting or boasting about his or her deviant behavior on these sites. The detectives are also gathering evidence from videos, pictures, and comments that are being posted by suspects and their friends on sites like YouTube. The ability to gain insight into the mentality of a possible suspect is increased when detectives monitor his or her posts and is especially easy when they set up a fake account to befriend the suspect. When such posts are available online, they are prone to be scrutinized and police officials can gain valuable intelligence on the suspected perpetrators, pre- and post-crime.

Interesting cases that validate the use of social media in catching criminals

- The New York City Police arrested a man last year on charges of murder after uncovering some incriminating posts on Facebook. This was the case of Melvin Colon, who faced murder charges and was also booked for crimes related to narcotics and illegal weapons. He was a suspect as a notorious New York City gang member. He posted some pictures on Facebook's public domain, flashing signs representing his gang and made many incriminating remarks in Facebook posts, hinting to violent crimes he had committed in the past. He also gave threats to various people among other posts. The Fourth Amendment application was debated hotly in this particular case of Colon. His lawyers claimed that all of Colon's posts on Facebook were under the full protection of the Fourth Amendment. This Amendment protects the effects and the homes of people from seizures and searches that can be deemed unreasonable. But a federal judge overruled his attorneys' argument stating that Colon had forfeited his privacy and his expectation of it when he shared the posts on Facebook with his friends.

- Another interesting example of social media being used to gather public data could be found in Cincinnati where the police took apart a street gang and booked more than seventy people six years ago. The investigation was a nine-month operation and it used so-

271

cial media in the identification of the local gang's key members. The police generated a database of valuable information derived from social networks and by collaborating with Cincinnati's Institute of Crime Science. It took its existing departmental and phone records and used software to analyze the data to establish a link between the suspects.

- In 2008, Ronnie Tienda Junior of Texas was charged with a murder that was gang related. This was largely possible because of some incriminating words and pictures that he had posted on the public domain pages of MySpace.

- Facebook made it clear to CNN that they have made no provisions for a law enforcement agency or a federal investigator to gain a backdoor access to their network. If the police want private information from Facebook, they will have to go through official channels to retrieve it. Every social network like Facebook, Twitter, LinkedIn, or MySpace has a policy on how it will divulge information when it is requested. A subpoena may be required based on the kind of information that is requested and also on the period for which that data has been hosted on the network. For example, in 2006, when the police suspected a Minnesota man named Darrin Anderson of communicating with underage girls using a fake Facebook account, they had to produce a search warrant for that particular profile. Facebook then handed over data of almost two and a half years from that profile which included more than eight hundred chat dialogues, mainly with girls who were under eighteen years of age. This profile on Facebook was later presented as evidence in court. The accused pleaded guilty to the charges of intent to illicit conduct of a sexual nature and he was sentenced to twelve years in prison.

- This is an exceptional case of tracking down a criminal. A British man was involved in the theft of jewelry worth $130,000. He fled the country after stealing those jewels. He returned back to the United Kingdom on vacation many months later under an assumed identity. He made one elementary error; he posted pictures of some of the jewelry that he had stolen on Facebook. The police officials, while closely watching social media for details on this suspect, managed to identify the photos of the stolen jewelry and tracked him down.

- Sometimes, the methods adopted by the law enforcement agencies do not stop at mere monitoring; they would even go as far as interacting with suspects. Police officers in Brooklyn set a trap and snared a gang of young people known as 'Brower Boys Gang.' The police officers added the members of these gangs as their friends on Facebook and were accepted. They followed all the crimes of the gang members as a result of their bragging on Facebook. Some of the gang members even hinted at their plans to commit burglary in their status update. They were trailed by the police, arrested, and jailed.

- In 2011, the Vancouver Police Department relied heavily on Twitter when riots broke out during the Stanley Cup finals. The Police Department posted tweets that were light in nature at the start of the series in a big community outreach attempt and these tweets were quite well received by their followers. The social media officer relied on Hoot Suite to gauge the public sentiment. When the riots broke out, the police department in Vancouver did not stop continuing with the tweets and they even used a trending hashtag, #canucksriot, to track the chaos. The Police Department gained so much popularity that their followers grew by almost 2,000 percent as people began to seek out information from them. After the riots, the Vancouver Police Department continued to use social media sites to make it easy for the residents to give tips about any illegal or unwarranted behavior. The quality of responses they received was tremendous. Never before in the history of the Vancouver city administration did the Police Department receive this type of response. Local journalists and residents submitted strong evidence of suspects who incited and triggered the riots. The public not only submitted photos to the Police Department, but they sent many tweets supporting the police.

Fake accounts are not allowed. But media sites are bending the rules.
Many law enforcement agency personnel have violated policies on Facebook and Twitter and created fake profiles in order to get friendly with suspects. Many police department officials are looking at vast public

information on all these media platforms and forums. They are also creating fake identities online to become friends with suspects to view all the information on their timelines. Authorities are also requesting private information directly from the social media channels by means of warrants and subpoenas. They occasionally make emergency requests for user information where they feel that there is a danger.

Police personnel all over the world have started using sites like Facebook to help victims identify the perpetrators of crime and suspects... basically an online mug shot book. Some police have started adopting a controversial approach for getting information out of the social network channels by going undercover and opening fake profiles so that they can sneak up and befriend the suspects. A report has revealed that almost ten percent of Facebook profiles are not genuine. These types of profiles may be violating the rules of the social network channels but they cannot be deemed wholly illegal. Evidence that is gathered by the police or law enforcement agencies in this way can

277

be upheld in a court of law. The LexisNexis survey revealed that most officials of law enforcement agencies had no problems when opening accounts with fake profiles for the purpose of investigation. Most officials feel opening fake accounts is completely ethical if the purpose is to hunt criminals.

In cases of emergencies where there is a credible and violent threat, authorities will not think twice about gaining instant access to any suspect's social network information. They will file for an emergency request. Recently, an anonymous post on Twitter led to unearthing a chain of tweets that talked about the threat of opening fire in a New York theater that was sponsoring a Broadway Show by Mike Tyson. One of the tweets talked about how a person had made a hit list out of the 600 people lined up for the show and bragged about how he could convert the event into a mass murder. Police detectives gave an emergency request to Twitter to come out with the full identity and details of the user. Twitter rejected that request on the grounds that it did not present sufficient evidence of an immediate threat.

The police finally brought a subpoena and Twitter was forced to comply with the emergency request and hand over the required information.

Most popular social media channels used by law enforcement agencies

A recent survey was conducted involving 1,200 law enforcement personnel on local, state, and federal levels in the United States that had used social media platforms as techniques to solve crimes. During the survey, four out of every five officers confirmed using social media to gather information and intelligence during their investigations. The majority of them acknowledged that social media had helped them solve their crimes much faster than ever before. This survey, organized by LexisNexis Risk Solutions, found that Facebook is the most widely used channel by law enforcement agencies. YouTube came next in popularity. Officials are using Facebook for leveraging and is just one many methods they use to gather evidence in solving crimes.

279

But not every criminal suspect will make it easy for law enforcement to track down his or her activities; yet, police strategies have evolved since the earlier days of Facebook. The methods adopted by private and public investigators have become more sophisticated in the last few years. Facebook has become one of the most fruitful sources for gathering criminal evidence. After Facebook began in 2005, it took some time for investigators and police officials to recognize the potential it possessed. College students mainly used Facebook in its early years. The police officials and campus authorities utilized Facebook to gather evidence towards violations of the alcohol policy at various colleges. Law enforcement officials started using Facebook for serious crimes in 2008 when the Cincinnati Police Department worked in unison with the University of Cincinnati to isolate vital gang members using Facebook posts. This was the first major case of police officers using social network channels to gather evidence against criminals.

Finding people through social media

Social media is not only used to help solve crimes but it is also used to find missing persons or people who may be in danger or in distress. User posts on social media sites give helpful insight into the mental state and intentions of missing people and possible suspects, leading to intelligent deductions. Through social media, officers of law enforcement agencies gather important clues on the whereabouts of people who may have simply run away from home or information on those people who are in distress and where they could be headed. Police are able to determine a fair idea about their plans by going through the posts, comments, likes, and lists of friends. Followers on Twitter could be asked to report on any kind of tips or warnings on crimes, suspected criminals who are on the loose, or missing persons.

Social networking and community outreach

A major step in solving crimes is taken when trust is established in a community. Police officials can achieve this objective by

RJ PARKER | JJ SLATE

generating an online presence of their own. Outlets of social media are able to take policing of communities to a higher level by offering cheap and fast ways to gather crucial information to the concerned citizens and investigators. Social media channels help project the police departments with a humanized angle by showing that the officers of these law enforcement agencies are community members too. This type of media has become an efficient vehicle for law enforcement agencies to bring to light the accomplishments of their officers and make relevant announcements concerning campaigns or other important messages about safety practices in the community.

Police are also prioritizing their public outreach and recruitment efforts with the help of social media. Today, there are Twitter accounts and Facebook pages for individual departments and the police officials use such forums to transmit important information to the people following them. For example, during the flooding in Queensland, Australia in 2011, the Facebook pages of the Police Department became a major source of regular updates, news, and warnings. The Department's Twitter feeds also became the primary source of communication for people on the go.

Using social media in hiring decisions

To establish trust in a community and to solve crimes, law enforcement agencies need a team of the right kind of people to work for them. They have to complete a comprehensive and extensive background check on all job applicants. MySpace and Facebook allow this type of background investigation to gain important insight into the character references of law enforcement candidates. With the help of networking sites like LinkedIn for professionals, officers and law enforcement agencies are able to obtain information from all over the world. This has encouraged review of the techniques employed by officers and has helped spread innovative ideas in law enforcement agencies. If you are considering a career in law enforcement, your actions today on social media may reflect whether you are hired or not.

Monitoring social media could cross boundaries

While hunting on Facebook has led to arrests, there have also been cases where some peaceful protesters and demonstrators have courted arrest because of their social media involvement and nosiness of the law enforcement agencies. For example, during the protests that were linked with Occupy Wall Street, a judge in New York City ruled that public tweets would not be considered in the same category as that of private speech and the court ordered Twitter to divulge all the deleted tweets from the accounts of some of the suspect protesters to be used as evidence in prosecuting them. There is always a possibility of police officials overstepping their boundaries of remaining undercover in various sting operations when they encroach on the entrapment terrain. While using social media, some officers could resort to blatant set-ups and they may also be cleared by the courts when adding suspects as friends. The ethical question comes to the forefront when some law enforcement officials actually *initiate* some criminal conversations and trap

284

the suspects only to rush through their cases. The police may have the upper hand in such discourses and may justify them as grounds for defense in entrapment cases.

Social media has such a phenomenal presence that it has become an indispensable part of the lives of several law enforcement officers. Use of social media brings both rewards and risks to the law enforcement officers and their departments. Any misuse could lead to criminal cases becoming compromised. However, the benefits of using social media channels outweigh any disadvantages they may present. Social media sites have grown exponentially. The Institute for Criminal Justice Education has reported that almost eighty percent of law enforcement officers held a profile or an account on social media channels. Almost all of them have the potential of using social media for crime prevention, investigation, and building up of public relations.

This mass jungle of electronic information has shown it can help law enforcement officers in apprehending fugitives, singling out all the suspects, linking suspects to gangs, and presenting any evidence of criminal activity.

Chapter 35: Internet Safety

How much of our lives do we spend planning for safety? From a very early age, we begin to learn the value of living life carefully. Toddlers learn not to touch things that will hurt them. We teach our children not to talk to strangers or to play with fire. When they grow a little older, it's time to explain to children the dangers of the street—how to look both ways before crossing the road, the meaning of streetlights, and how to ride their bikes in a safe manner. We teach them how to swim for the sake of water safety, to stay away from thin ice on the lake, and under no circumstances are they to answer the door to strangers when they are home alone. As time passes, children enter their teens, learn how to handle power tools in shop class, take driver's education classes to ensure safety behind the wheel of a car, and learn not to drink and drive all with the purpose of living life safely. Each generation brings with it new social settings, innovative technology, and a new set of rules to learn.

Over the decades, the rules have changed gradually, even foreseeably. Traditionally, it has been the responsibility of the adults in society to train younger generations about technology and safety on the journey to becoming productive citizens. With the invention of this mind-boggling phenomenon called the internet, though, all of the long-held, tried and true rules and strategies on which we have so comfortably relied upon have changed. There are new ways of doing things now that never in our wildest dreams could we have imagined would have been the case thirty years ago. If that weren't startling enough, the pace at which the internet continues to evolve is equally staggering. In fact, young people are often far more adept within the internet environment than are their parents…. Now there's an unsettling thought! The average person isn't even able to fully define what the internet is or how it originated and evolved. It could quite feasibly be described as this abstract, unimaginably massive, global setting where anyone and everyone can frequent without entirely understanding what they are doing. It is possible to find the answers to practically anything a mind could fathom, yet the fact remains that most of us really don't understand the full implications of our presence on the internet. How can we continue our societal duty and tradition of safe living when we don't even wholly comprehend what the internet is or the extent of its power? How can we, therefore, protect ourselves and our children in such a setting?

Educating ourselves would seem to be the first line of defense. It is said that in order to conquer something with the intention of bringing it into submission, one first must understand it. That's a fancy way of saying that to be safe on the internet, you must first learn what it is and how to make it work *for you*, as opposed to against you. It seems that the internet was an inevitable and reasonable progression following the invention of amazing technology such as the telegraph, telephone, radio, television, and computer. Imagine how society reacted at the introduction of each of these historic concepts. Today, we take for granted that great minds of our time will simply continue in this progressive direction. The first sign of the internet appeared in 1962 when Mr. J.C.R. Licklider of MIT foresaw "a globally interconnected set of computers through which everyone could quickly access data and programs from any site." At an extremely basic level of understanding, the first internet-like structure began in 1969 with the creation of the ARPANET (a network created by the United States Defense Advanced Research Project Agency), which linked numerous universities and research centers together. The technology continued to evolve and in 1974, computer researchers developed technology that allowed computers to "talk to each other." The World Wide Web was created in the 1990s as global networking continued to grow. Today, the internet is a global network of millions of computers with more than 100 countries linked in the exchange of information and nearly three billion users as of 2014. What does all this mean? It means that access to all kinds of information is at your fingertips, as well as the tips of billions of other fingers. It means that YOUR information may also be accessed by strangers if you don't take specific precautions.

So, who is at risk? Anyone who accesses the internet, of course. Children, youth, adults, and seniors are all targets on the internet when they go online unprepared. Obviously, each of those age groups is accessing the internet with different goals in mind. Children are usually online to play games and watch videos of their favorite shows or movies. Young people go online to meet up with their friends in chat rooms, Facebook, or Twitter, for gaming opportunities, YouTube, Netflix and so much more. They also know how to surf the net to help with homework assignments, study for exams, and research job opportunities and postsecondary schools. Adults use the internet for banking and financial reasons, to research business contacts, as a tool in their jobs, for leisure surfing and social networking, for online courses, blogging, and so on. The list is endless. And then there are seniors. Seniors are accessing the internet more and more. Their interests seem to lie in researching health issues, government websites, for financial activities, such as banking and investments, leisure surfing, hobbies, blog writing, and even social networking. Because of the vastly different uses of the internet from age group to age group, online safety will require different strategies.

Children are such trusting individuals. Unfortunately, the days where our safety advice consisted of "Don't talk to strangers," "Don't eat sweets before supper," and "Look both ways before crossing the street" are over. Most children have access to the internet at least some of the time. Their lack of life experience usually leaves them ill prepared for those inappropriate sites that inevitably pop up online. Further, they tend to think they are invincible and that no one could ever hurt them. They don't realize the seriousness of the existence of predators that lurk online, waiting for opportunities to lure them in. Parents do have options for protecting their children and must stick to very specific online rules. Here are some rules to help:

- Place your computer in a visible area of the house in order to monitor what sites your children are visiting.
- Monitor the internet history of the computer regularly to check on web addresses your children have accessed. This includes ALL internet-capable devices at their disposal (iPads, iPhones, etc.).
- Establish a "no browser history erase" rule: break the rule = no more internet use.
- Choose one of the kid-safe search engines as your default setting on

your web browser page:
- o www.kidoz.net/plus/index.html (for four-year-olds)
- o www.kids.aol.com/KOL/1/KOLJr (for five-year-olds)
- o www.kidinfo.com (for six-year-olds)
- o www.askforkids.com (for six-year-olds)
- o www.kidsclick.org (for eight-year-olds)
- o www.zoodles.com (for eight-year-olds)
- o www.sweetsearch.com (for thirteen-year-olds)
- o www.scholar.google.com (for fifteen-year-olds)

- Establish and regularly review a set of family rules for internet use, such as:
  - o Appropriate time of day to be online.
  - o Amount of time to use the computer per session.
  - o Always have parental consent

to go online.
- o Create a list of off-limits sites.
- o Kids must immediately report to parents any inappropriate sites they accidentally access.
- Limit instant messaging and emailing to a parent-approved 'buddy list.'
- Surf the internet together to establish a bookmarked list of sites based on your child's interests.
- Know your child's usernames and passwords.
- Discuss with your child the difference between private and public information. Point out the dangers of providing a home address or phone number, or even revealing one's hometown. This is when you should be discussing the existence of online predators and how they operate:
  - o Someone posing as a child could actually be an adult try-

ing to gain information from you.

o Online predators will often lie to you in an effort to gain your trust... They'll agree with you on pretty much anything to connect with you.

o They will ask for your name, age, gender, and other specific information about yourself.

o A fake online name is best, as opposed to your real name. At the very most, use only your first name. No one should be asking you for more information than that.

o Never enter your real name, age, address, or phone number online. Predators can use that information to locate other personal information.

o Be very careful if someone online asks to meet with you in person. Tell an adult immediately! DO NOT MEET SOMEONE YOU MET ONLINE IN PERSON!

o The internet is not a place to make new friends. Online relationships can be dangerous. (Establish a rule where your children must report to you any new people they have met online and monitor conversations closely.)

• Discuss with your child the realities of pornography and, most important, child pornography. They need to understand that child pornography is ALWAYS ILLEGAL and must be reported for their safety, as well as the safety of other children.

• Discuss the concept of cyberbullying: what it is, how it happens, and how to conduct oneself online. Explain to your child that gossiping, harassment, humiliation, threats, etc., constitute cyberbullying, which is ILLEGAL. Explain the repercussions of such online activity: how it affects the victims, retaliation measures taken by the victims, legal implications, and how death has resulted in certain cases.

- If your child is the victim of cyberbullying, encourage him or her to confide in you. Do not overreact. Instead, discuss the situation with your child to determine the seriousness of the incident. Is it simply annoying contact, or does it involve imminent emotional and/or physical abuse? You can alert your child's school to be watchful of bullying activity involving your child and ask them to take particular note of how your child is handling the situation. You can also inform your family physician and clergy of what is happening and seek guidance from those perspectives. Above all, TAKE THIS SERIOUSLY. Cyberbullying can result in irreparable, long-lasting harm. Refer to *Beyond Sticks and Stones: Bullying* by RJ Parker for more information.

Adults, on the other hand, should know better, yet considering this mysterious environment in which we now find ourselves, it's not surprising that most of us really don't know better. We have our own set of safety precautions to follow that are more suited to the online risks we face, but without educating ourselves on the matter, how can we implement said precautions? One area of risk for adults revolves around identity theft, which is why the utmost care must be taken to avoid revealing personal information online. One statistic reveals that victims of identity theft lost a total of $7 billion in 2012 alone. Businesses are also at risk losing an estimated $44 billion in that same year…. These are staggering numbers. It can be an arduous task to restore your identity and repair your reputation. What's worse is that once your identity has been stolen, you are even more of a target for future theft because so much of your identification doesn't change. Yes, you can cancel credit cards and bank accounts, change your address, change usernames and passwords, but your name, age, birthdate, place of birth, mother's maiden name, and so on will not change. This information has already been discovered and recorded by a criminal element with the potential to be reused at a later date. As such, you must make a conscientious effort to protect yourself. All is not lost though. There are various measures available to protect yourself when online:

- Research the privacy settings of social networking sites.
- Ask family and friends to examine your social networking sites, watching for personal information or inappropriate photos or videos that you may have missed.

- Do not share your usernames and passwords with anyone.
- Respect yourself and others while online.
- Everyone over the age of fourteen should be monitoring their credit history on a regular basis. You can request a credit history report from a number of sources or even hire a credit monitoring service to keep an eye on things for you.
- Request a credit disclosure from one of the three national credit reporting organizations: TransUnion, Equifax, or Experian. These three organizations created AnnualCreditReport.com, which is a service to help consumers obtain a free annual report.
- Decide whether or not you want your personal information accessible in online directory searches. You can limit access to your information or keep it private entirely,

usually for a fee called a "privacy tax."

- Obviously, if your identity has been stolen, contact all of your banking and financial institutions immediately, as well as your insurance company and local law enforcement. Remember to freeze your credit with all three of the preceding credit reporting organizations.
- If damaging images or videos of you have been exposed online, contacting the website where they appeared will likely result in their removal and possibly even disciplinary measures for the offender.
- It is also a good idea to notify family and friends of the theft in the event that they might be affected as well.
- Keep your usernames, passwords, and PINs secure and change them often. Never use the same

username and password for multiple sites, as this will have a domino effect throughout your accounts if one of the accounts is compromised.

- When creating a new password, use a combination of letters (both uppercase and lowercase), numbers, and symbols. The more complicated you make the combination, the more difficult it will be for criminals to decode it.
- PIN numbers should not be phone numbers, birthdates, or sequential or repeating numbers.
- Social networks are open to the whole world. Be careful not to include personal information on your profile and never accept friend requests from strangers.
- When using public computers (at the library, internet cafes, etc.), do not conduct identity sensitive business such as online banking, do not

save usernames and passwords, ALWAYS clear your browser history, and be aware of anyone looking over your shoulder.

- Ensure that your computer is firewall-, antivirus-, and malware-protected. There is a variety of software programs available for purchase or as free downloads that serve this purpose.

Senior presence on the internet is a rapidly growing trend and, as with any other group, requires the practice of online safety. It is inaccurate to stereotype all older people as seniors who are scared to use technology. In fact, many seniors are avid internet users. They surf, blog, research, take courses, pay their bills, and do so much more online. On the other hand, there are those seniors who are more traditional and still uncomfortable with how to operate certain types of technology. For some, the concept of a computer is a significant source of confusion, and the internet is unimaginable. They, too, must learn the new rules of this information age that will keep them safe while enjoying the fascination of the internet.

The internet can open up a whole new dimension in life for seniors who often become isolated and out of touch as they age. Our jobs, careers, and professions are frequently a defining force in our lives. Once retirement becomes a reality, seniors can feel a need to continue to be productive. They miss the intellectual stimulation and challenges of their work life. That fast, relentless pace of working, raising a family, of never having enough hours in the day can eventually become too many unfulfilling hours with not enough to do. More and more seniors are discovering the world of the internet where virtually anything they've ever wanted to know is just a few clicks away. It has become a rich intellectual source where they can continue to learn and grow as individuals.

Areas where seniors need to be educated

and remain aware are:
- Phishing: these are online scams that try to convince you they are trusted, legitimate companies. They often take the form of official bank notices or government forms and documents. They look like the real thing but actually end up tricking the recipient into disclosing personal information.
- Lack of computer skills: seniors tend to be less familiar with operating a computer, so they need to either learn to equip their computers with firewall- and antivirus-protection or else ask someone they trust to set up their security for them.
- Lack of internet skills: computer skills and internet skills are two different things. Where computer skills refer to the actual technology of the machine, internet skills involve understanding human nature and how people can use the internet to exploit others. Exposure to the internet will teach seniors when

to click and when not to click, how to recognize scams, and the potential for criminal targeting.

- Seniors are usually more trusting and may believe a notice sent out to them stating that there is a problem with one of their accounts. Be very leery of notices asking for personal information. Contact your account institutions directly regarding the validity of such notices.

- Emails from unfamiliar sources should be deleted immediately. Opening the wrong emails can introduce viruses, which can then spread and compromise your computer and identity.

- Advanced Fee Letter Fraud (Nigerian or West African letters): these are email scams that offer you a considerable amount of money to help someone transfer a huge sum of money. They state that they can't get the money out of a certain country and offer to share the money with you if you let them use your bank account to transfer the money. Once you provide them with your bank account number, they can access the account and withdraw your money.

- Malicious Software: Viruses, worms, Trojan horse programs, spyware, and adware are a real threat and can infect your computer simply by clicking on fraudulent emails. Be careful not to open emails from unfamiliar sources. Remember: if something looks too good to be true, it probably is.

The internet with its infinite possibilities is an incredible achievement of mankind. It can be a source of immeasurable benefit, but it can also be an avenue for great harm. Protection from such harm can only be achieved through education of its perils and through diligent monitoring. Discovery has never been easier. Disaster can be just as easy if you aren't careful. Whether riding your bike down a busy city street for the first time or cruising around the internet in search of knowledge, caution must be foremost in your mind.

This chapter included basic safety rules that many are already taking precautions against. There is one particular feature on Facebook that I am dubious about and that is the ability to "check in" at certain locations. People are using this feature to let their friends know they are at a restaurant, or the mall, the swimming pool, etc., but they are also letting potential stalkers and criminals know as well. This feature essentially gives away your exact GPS location. My GPS on my iPhone is turned on only for maps and weather. Why does the entire world need to know where you are located?

This book has only been a small sample guiding you through the brutality of a killer's mind. Hundreds of other different types of killers can be found throughout history. These combined true stories can bring a better understanding to the diverted nature of a human being.

As you may have noticed, committing a murder is more complicated than the mere act. Many of the reasons that drive a person to kill someone else can be traced as far back as to the childhood of that person. Troubled childhoods, verbal abuse, but mostly sexual abuse, are all factors that contribute into the making of a killer. Although the motives of a killer are not always logical, some do not understand the gravity of their actions, even after they are put away.

In the stories chosen for this book, often the families of the victims were able to have some kind of closure, even though they still lost their loved ones. Others were not so lucky. Not only did the murderers take the lives of their loved ones, they also inflicted pain and misery to their families and friends.

As the final words in this book are written, we hope that it will make a good contribution and reference to the criminal history of mankind, mainly of modern killers who depend on today's technology to commit crimes.

THANK YOU for purchasing and reading our book,
Social Media Monsters: Internet Killers. We are truly blessed to have such a supportive community of fans and readers. Often people ask us is there is anything else they can do to support us as authors. We would be so appreciative if you would take the time to write a brief review of this book at the place you bought it online. Reviews are so important to authors and hearing from our readers simply never gets old. Thank you for your support!

Blessings,

RJ Parker and JJ Slate

 **RJ PARKER**, P.Mgr., CIM, is an award-winning and bestselling true crime author, and serial killer expert, most well known for his books: *TOP CASES of The FBI, Serial Killer Case Files,* and *Cold Blooded Killers.* He writes most of his books exclusively for Amazon.

RJ Parker was born and raised in Newfoundland and now resides in Ontario and Newfoundland, Canada. Parker started writing after becoming disabled with Anklyosing Spondylitis. He spent twenty-five years in various facets of Government and has two professional designations.

To date, RJ has donated over 2,000 books to allied troops serving overseas and to our wounded warriors recovering in Naval and Army hospitals all over the world. He also donates a percentage of royalties to Victims of Violent Crimes.

CONTACT INFORMATION

Website: www.RJParkerPublishing.com
Email: AuthorRJParker@gmail.com
Email: Agent@RJParkerPublishing.com
Amazon:
www.amazon.com/author/rjparkertruecrime
Twitter: www.twitter.com/AuthorRJParker
Facebook:
www.facebook.com/RJParkerPublishing

RJ Parker's Bibliography

- ***Social Media Monsters: Internet Killers*** – 18 September 2014
  eBook / Paperback /Paperback Large Print / Audiobook
- ***Serial Killers Abridged*** - 31 May 2014
  eBook / Paperback / Audiobook
- ***Parents Who Killed Their Children*** - 30 April 2014
  eBook / Paperback / Audiobook
- ***Beyond Sticks and Stones*** - 14 March 2014
  eBook / Paperback / Audiobook
- ***Serial Killers True Crime Anthology 2014, Vol. I*** -
  14 December 2013
  eBook / Paperback / Paperback Large Print / Audiobook
- ***Cold Blooded Killers*** - 30 November 2013
  eBook / Paperback / Audiobook
- ***Serial Killers Case Files*** - 15 June 2013
  eBook / Paperback / Audiobook

- ***Case Closed: Serial Killers Captured*** - 24 October 2012
  eBook / Paperback / Audiobook
- ***Doctors Who Killed*** - 24 October 2012
  eBook / Paperback / Audiobook
- ***Rampage: Spree Killers*** - 24 October 2012
  eBook / Paperback / Audiobook
- ***Women Who Kill*** - 11 November 2011
  eBook / Paperback / Audiobook
- ***Unsolved Serial Killings*** - 01 August 2011
  eBook / Audiobook
- ***Top Cases of the FBI*** - 05 May 2012
  eBook / Paperback / Audiobook
- ***Serial Killer Compendium*** - 05 June 2012
  Audiobook

JJ SLATE is a best-selling true crime author and blogger. Born in Massachusetts, she has always been fascinated with true crime stories, especially those dealing with missing persons and cold cases. This is JJ's second book with RJ Parker Publishing, Inc. Her first, *Missing Wives, Missing Lives*, a compilation of true cases about wives that have gone missing, published in June of 2014 and quickly became an Amazon bestseller. She has several more books in the works for 2015 and 2016.

JJ currently lives in New England with her husband. When she isn't writing or researching her next book, she is usually blogging about current cases in the media.

CONTACT INFORMATION

Blog: www.jenniferjslate.com
Email: JJSlate@RJParkerPublishing.com
Amazon: www.amazon.com/author/jjslate
Twitter: www.twitter.com/jenniferjslate
Facebook: www.facebook.com/JJSlate